Deep South Parties

Robert St. John

Deep South Parties

or

How to Survive the Southern Cocktail Hour Without a Box of French-Onion Soup Mix, a Block of Processed Cheese, or a Cocktail Weenie

A Cookbook Featuring the New Celebratory Cuisine of the South with Recollections and Stories from the Region

HYPERION

New York

Book design by Nicola Ferguson

Library of Congress Cataloging-in-Publication Data
St. John, Robert
Deep south parties or, How to survive the Southern cocktail hour without a box of French onion soup mix, a block of processed cheese, or a cocktail weenie : a cookbook featuring the new celebratory cuisine of the South with recollections and stories from the region / Robert St. John.
p. cm.
ISBN 1-4013-0840-6
1. Cookery, American—Southern style. 2. Entertaining. I. Title.
TX715.2.S68S6623 2006
641.5975—dc22   2006041245

Hyperion books are available for special promotions and premiums. For details contact Michael Rentas, Manager, Inventory and Premium Sales, Hyperion, 77 West 66th Street, 12th floor, New York, New York 10023, or call 212-456-0133.

1   3   5   7   9   10   8   6   4   2

For Jill–

She knows why

Contents

List of Illustrations

Photos on pp. ii, x, xiv, xvi, 10, 19, 27, 28, 52, 57, 60, 64, 65, 75, 85, 86, 95, 98, 109, 110, 113, 116, 125, 130, 135, 142, 145, 156, 165, 166, 180, 200, 214, 216, 218, 223, 233: H. Armstrong Roberts/Classicstock

Photo on pp. xxi and 213: Ewing Galloway/Camerique Inc./Classicstock

Photos on p xxii: Voller Ernst/Classicstock

Photos on pp. 30 and 31: Margaret Ewing/Classicstock

Photo on p. 34: Wisconsin Historical Society/Classicstock

Photo on p. 49: American Stock Photography/Classicstock

Photo on p. 60: C. P. Cushing/Classicstock

Photo on p. 104: Benelux Press/Classicstock

Photo on p. 148: Popperfoto/Classicstock

Photo on p. 177: Lambert Studios/Classicstock

Photo on p. 192: David W. Corson/Classicstock

Photo on p. 238: R. Kord/Classicstock

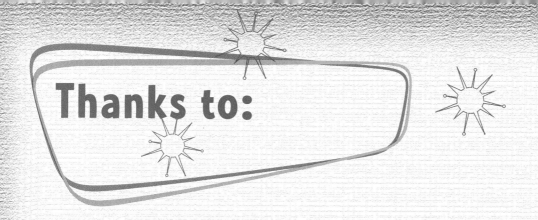

Thanks to:

Jill, Holleman, and Harrison for being there for me, and letting me be there for the book. Thanks guys, for loaning me out for a few months.

Linda Nance—chef, recipe tester, friend, and fellow hurricane survivor—for the very early mornings and extremely long kitchen hours spent in the five months after the worst natural disaster ever to hit American soil.

Barbara Jane Foote—the most organized person I know—for sharing her thoughts, ideas, recipes, and party memories.

Mitchell Waters, agent, for getting it done.

Will Schwalbe, for his belief in me and my work.

Leslie Wells, Miriam Wenger, Allison McGeehon, and the Hyperionites for endless patience, guidance, and for not strangling me every time I deserved it.

Julia Reed, fellow food lover, for an outstanding foreword, friendship, and Delta wit.

The staff and management of the Purple Parrot Café, Crescent City Grill, and Mahogany Bar in Hattiesburg and Meridian, Mississippi.

The loyal restaurant customers and weekly column readers.

Introduction

Recipe testing for this book was set to begin September 1, 2005. On the morning of August 29, Hurricane Katrina made landfall one hour due south of my hometown and for several hours, the Eastern-eye wall carrying winds of up to 130 miles per hour pounded my house, office, restaurants, and neighbors. When the storm had ceased and the veil of initial shock was lifted, my neighborhood, my town, and my little region of the country looked a lot different.

The storm blew the second-floor balcony off of one of my restaurants and sent six five-ton air-conditioning units tossing and tumbling across the roof of another. Twenty-seven trees fell on or around my house. In an instant, we were living in a disaster area of Old Testament proportions.

Two days after the storm, I was sitting in my pitch-dark house eating a sandwich. It was a sandwich made of cheap, pressed luncheon meat, white bread, and Creole mustard. Sitting in the heat amid the rubble, that simple meal might as well have been prime aged New York strip with foie gras and truffles. Actually, it might have tasted better than any steak has ever tasted. It was at that precise moment that it struck me . . . Creole mustard is a beautiful thing.

Creole mustard, unadorned. No elaborate seasoning on the meat, nothing artisan about the bread, nothing complicated at all, just whole-grain mustard. Simple, easy, uncomplicated. As life should be, as life could be, again.

The lessons learned were:

1. Never take food for granted, no matter how simple or easy.
2. Slow down and enjoy every meal—and each component of every meal.

3. Never underestimate the value of electricity.
4. The taproot of the Southern yellow pine was not made to withstand 130 mph winds.

After a few weeks, electricity was restored, and work on the book began. The storm fostered in me a new resolve, and served as a lightning rod and springboard from which to start the recipe-testing phase of this book.

It turns out that the worst storm ever to strike mainland America had no effect on the outcome of this project, other than to strengthen my determination to pro-

duce a volume of recipes and writings that would endure the taste-tests of time, ones that I would be proud to share with others who love the party foods of the Deep South.

This is my third cookbook. The recipes listed herein represent foods—new and old—which make up the celebratory cuisine of the Deep South.

My weekly food column is usually pegged as a "food/humor column." I rarely get serious when I write about food. Though there are humorous essays in this manuscript, the food is seriously good and the recipes are solid.

This volume will sit on my cookbook shelf and serve as the definitive entertaining guide for me and my family. I hope that it serves the same purpose for you and yours.

I count my blessings every day. I have a wonderful wife, two amazing children, I eat for a living, and I don't have to wear a tie when I go to work. Life is good.

Robert St. John
Hattiesburg, Mississippi
January 15, 2006

Foreword

When I was in college in Washington, D.C., I decided to throw a party during Ronald Reagan's first inaugural. The guest list included my colleagues at *Newsweek* (where my primary duties involved answering the phone and theirs involved reporting actual stories) and a lot of other folks equally older than I and much cooler, all of whom I desperately wanted to impress. I got my hands on the *Russian Tea Room Cookbook* so I could replicate their "Eggplant Orientale" dip to the last ingredient. I bought real French cheeses at the gourmet market and spent all my meager earnings on the tenderloin with homemade yeast rolls that was always a staple on my mother's party table. And then, hours before the event, when I was halfway through a recipe I'd found in *Vogue* for Choux Paste Puffs Stuffed with Smoked Whitefish Salad, the doorbell rang. It was the driver of the celebrated Georgetown hostess Susan Mary Alsop, and he was holding one grocery bag loaded with boxes of frozen La Choy miniature egg rolls and another with Stouffer's French bread pizzas (accompanied by instructions from Susan Mary to cut them into strips). Mrs. Alsop, he said, was terribly sorry she couldn't make it to the party, but she wanted to send something along.

My boarding school roommate, who had been to cooking school in France and who had come up to help me with the party, was floored. We had spent the majority of our friendship working on how to look and act like sophisticated thirty-five-year-olds and now here was this man in a chauffeur's cap offering up some dorm party staples from no less a grande dame than Mrs. Alsop. My friend was highly insulted, but I knew better. Susan Mary routinely served the same stuff to ambassadors and cabinet members at her own house.

Of course, there was a big difference between Susan Mary and me. She was a direct descendant of John Jay, one of the signers of the Declaration of Independence; the ex-lover of Duff Cooper, the charismatic British diplomat; and the ex-wife of Joseph Alsop, the powerful American columnist who was himself a close cousin of Franklin Roosevelt and an intimate of John F. Kennedy. (It was to Joe and Susan Mary's house that Kennedy had come after his own inaugural ball.) She had lived in Paris, written three books, wore Balmain and Valentino couture. She was also a Yankee with the physique of a baby sparrow and not the least bit interested in food. I knew this because for a time I was lucky enough to be the "young thing" meant to lighten up her rather heavy guest list. One nerve-wracking evening, when I found myself seated between Caspar Weinberger and Brent Scowcroft, we all munched on cold roast beef accompanied only by salad and toasted pita bread triangles while I tried hard to think of something amusing to say. The food was never the point—people were too busy parsing Henry Kissinger's latest volume of memoirs (he was a frequent guest) or engaging in world-class gossip.

In the many years since that inaugural effort, I have entertained a few cabinet members and ambassadors myself, though I have yet to serve anyone frozen egg rolls or pizza at a party. Maybe I'll never be that secure, or maybe it's a Southern thing. Maybe I just love to watch the happy faces of guests when they bite into a fried oyster or a deviled egg or a big dollop of jumbo lump crab salad on toast. Maybe I think really delicious food fuels conversation, even—or especially—that which involves affairs of state. Whatever the case, as much as I admired the late great Susan Mary in almost every way, it has always been my mother on whom I've relied for advice on what to serve when I entertain. Now, thank heaven, we both have Robert St. John.

I cannot express strongly enough what a valuable service Robert has performed in writing this book. I entertain a lot, a whole lot, and there are only so many times you can put out platters of the same deviled eggs, the same sliced tenderloin, or the same crabmeat salad, no matter how fabulous. I have pored over hundreds of cookbooks and magazines, trying to come up with something—anything—new in the way of hors d'oeuvres or canapés, but most are too tricky or a little weird (think of those puffs full of smoked whitefish). Now, finally, my good friend Robert has managed to tweak the grand old staples (seafood au gratin, crawfish cardinale) and come up with new ones that still fall into the category of what my mother has always simply referred to as "food that tastes good." In other words, food that is not too contrived or overwrought.

Susan Mary was definitely on to something—there is not a thing wrong with cold roast beef, it's just a tad spartan for us Southerners unless it is lavishly accompanied, as Robert accompanies his (which also happens to be smoked, naturally), with both chive and tarragon sauce and horseradish mustard. It can even be argued that La Choy egg rolls aren't bad things, but along those same lines I would rather eat—and happily serve without embarrassment—Robert's shrimp empanadas or miniature crawfish pies. Both are in a chapter called "Out of the Freezer," which points to the fact that people do drop in on each other in our neck of the woods and, when they do, you must have something available to offer them with their gin and tonics. "They'll wonder how you made something that tastes so good, and looks so complicated, so quickly," Robert says in his introduction to the Shrimp Empanadas recipe. Since there are very few Declaration signers lingering in most of our gene pools, we have learned to cook to impress.

Signers aside, Robert celebrates our own heritage with ample use of bacon grease; black-eyed peas (you will never eat hummus made with the lowly chickpea again); shrimp, crab, and crawfish; and, of course, pimento cheese, which he calls the "pâté of the South." There are no less than three recipes for the stuff, along with one for pimento cheese ham biscuits and another for miniature grilled pimento cheese sandwiches, which may well be the best things I've ever tasted.

The utterly mouthwatering recipes are matched by Robert's serious knowledge of how to entertain. My mother is a big afficionado of the cocktail supper, as are pretty much all the hostesses in the Mississippi Delta. That means that they all have parties with food plenty substantial enough to be a meal but you don't need a plate or utensils to eat it, thereby freeing up the guests' hands and valuable time (no standing in line, no getting a plate) so that we can get on with what most of us would rather be doing, which is drinking and socializing. When I moved to New York and sent out invitations to my first cocktail supper, people were completely thrown. They thought they were going to be forced to sit down and eat supper, which would preclude drop-bys. Or they thought there might be supper but no wine, only cocktails. I persisted and people finally got used to it, especially after they tasted the food, which did not include the usual Manhattan cocktail fare of dried-up chicken satay on a stick and undercooked snow peas piped with fish paste.

Anyway, almost every single recipe in this book is perfect for a cocktail supper—even the desserts. Robert has managed, for example, to come up with strawberry shortcakes you can eat in one bite, as well as divine miniature fried peach pies. He also understands the global nature of the way the best Southern hosts and hostesses entertain. There are chapters called "To Be Passed," "On the Sideboard," "Buffet Table," and my favorite, "Around and About the House." Who among us wouldn't have a bowl of sugared peanuts on, say, the bar, and a plate of fiery cheese straws on the piano?

There is, in fact, nothing in this book I wouldn't have. I thought I'd eaten all the tired-old hot artichoke dip I ever wanted until I tasted Robert's with the addition of oysters and Creole seasoning; I thought I knew every topping there was for that old standby, the block of cream cheese, until I discovered his peach preserves spiced with cayenne and chili flakes and paprika. Every recipe in the book is a gift—and not just to lucky guests, but to hostesses like me who desperately needed an updated repertoire and a glorious new reason to throw a party.

—Julia Reed

Deep South Parties

To Be Passed

Sweet-Potato Nachos with Boursin, Pecans, and Roasted Red Peppers

Red-Bean-and-Rice Spring Rolls with Creole-Tomato Dipping Sauce

Parmesan-Panko–Crusted Eggplant with Comeback Dipping Sauce

Crispy-Fried Oyster BLTs

Shrimp Toast with Plum Dipping Sauce

Crab Fritters with Seafood Rémoulade Sauce

Chicken Skewers with Georgia-Peanut Dipping Sauce

Black-and-Blue Nachos

Lamb Kebabs with Raspberry-Mint Dipping Sauce

Bloody-Mary Oyster Shooters

Crabmeat Puffs with Pepper-Jelly Dipping Sauce

Coconut Shrimp with Muscadine Dipping Sauce

Crawfish-Andouille Hush Puppies

Mushroom-Stuffed Pastry

Miniature Grilled Pimento-Cheese Sandwiches

Sweet-Potato Nachos with Boursin, Pecans, and Roasted Red Peppers Yield: 10-12 servings

This recipe has the perfect blend of flavors, colors, and textures. Make sure that the chips are fried crispy. Floppy chips can't hold the topping. Always use a deep-fat thermometer when frying so you can regulate the temperature of the oil.

1 large sweet potato, sliced into very thin potato-chip-like circles

Peanut oil for frying

1 cup Boursin cheese (page 137)

½ cup roasted red peppers, cut into 1½-inch-long strips

½ cup pecan pieces, toasted

1 Tbl fresh chives, chopped

1. Using a deep-fat thermometer to check the temperature, preheat about 1 inch of oil to 325 degrees in a cast-iron skillet.

2. Fry the sweet-potato chips 6–7 at a time. Move the chips often and cook to a light brown color. Drain onto paper towels.

3. Preheat oven to 325 degrees.

4. Once drained, place the chips on a baking sheet. Top each slice with 2 tsp Boursin cheese and 3 strips of roasted pepper. Bake 3 minutes.

5. Sprinkle with toasted pecans and chives and serve immediately.

Red-Bean-and-Rice Spring Rolls with Creole-Tomato Dipping Sauce

Yield: 18-20 spring rolls

Red beans and rice are a New Orleans Monday-lunch staple. I wanted to develop a way to serve them as a finger food at a stand-up cocktail party. In the end, I might like this version better than the sit-down original.

Peanut oil for frying

2 cups cooked red beans

1 package egg-roll wrappers (18–20 per package)

1½ cups white rice, steamed

Egg wash (1 egg beaten with 2 Tbl water)

1. Using a deep-fat thermometer to check the temperature, heat about 1 inch of oil to 350 degrees.

2. Place red beans in a food processor and pulse mixture briefly to roughly purée the beans.

3. Lay egg-roll wrapper on a flat surface. Follow the manufacturer's directions on the egg roll wrapper's label for filling, using 1½ Tbl of the red-bean mixture and 1 Tbl of the steamed white rice. Seal egg roll with egg wash.

4. Fry in small batches until golden brown. Drain on paper towels and cut on the bias. Serve with Creole-Tomato Dipping Sauce (page 186).

Don't "force" a party. Wait until you are ready to entertain.

TIP for Entertaining

3

Parmesan-Panko-Crusted Eggplant with Comeback Dipping Sauce

Yield: 25-30 sticks

When prepared correctly, there is a buttery quality to the eggplant in this recipe. These should be served immediately. Comeback Sauce (page 196) is the perfect accompaniment; the Pepper-Jelly Dipping Sauce (page 182) would work well, too. Panko bread crumbs are also called Japanese bread crumbs. They are perfect for this recipe, as they add texture and crunch.

1 large eggplant, cut into 3-inch-long squared sticks
   (3 inches x ½ inch x ½ inch, about the size of a forefinger)
1 Tbl kosher salt
Vegetable or peanut oil for frying

1 cup seasoned flour (page 208)
1 cup egg wash (3 eggs beaten with ¼ cup water)
1½ cups panko bread crumbs
1 cup Parmesan cheese, freshly grated
1 Tbl parsley, finely chopped
2 tsp black pepper, freshly ground

TIP for Entertaining

Limit the number of appetizers on each tray so they will stay neat. Refill frequently.

1. Place cut-up eggplant in a colander and sprinkle with the kosher salt. Allow the eggplant to drain for one hour.

2. Using a deep-fat thermometer to check the temperature, preheat about 1 inch of oil in a fryer or deep cast-iron skillet to 350 degrees.

3. Three-bowl breading procedure: Place seasoned flour in the first bowl, egg wash in the second, and bread crumbs, cheese, parsley, and black pepper in the third.

4. Dredge eggplant sticks in the flour, shaking off excess. Dip into egg wash, then into bread crumb mixture. Coat eggplant sticks thoroughly.

5. Fry eggplant sticks 4–6 at a time until golden brown. Place on paper towels to drain. Serve with Comeback Sauce (page 196) or Pepper-Jelly Dipping Sauce (page 182).

Crispy-Fried Oyster BLTs

I first ate these when my friend Julia Reed served them at a cocktail party in the courtyard of her Bourbon Street home. Make sure to use small oysters so that they can be eaten in one or two bites.

FRIED OYSTERS

Peanut oil for frying

1⅔ cups cornmeal

⅓ cup corn flour

2 tsp salt

2 Tbl Creole seasoning (page 205)

2 dozen oysters, freshly shucked

4–5 whole leaves romaine lettuce

1 cup Seafood Rémoulade Sauce (page 191)

½ cup bacon, cooked and chopped

TIP for Entertaining

To avoid mealy critters—and to preserve freshness and flavor-store ground cornmeal in a tightly sealed plastic bag in the freezer.

1. Using a deep-fat thermometer to check the temperature, heat oil in cast-iron skillet to 350 degrees.

2. Combine cornmeal, corn flour, salt, and Creole seasoning. Drop oysters into cornmeal mixture and drop one at a time into hot oil. Fry until golden and crispy (approximately 5 minutes), remove, drain.

3. To assemble the BLTs: Cut two-inch-wide sections from the romaine leaves. Cut across the leaves so that each piece has a center rib piece.

4. Place 2 tsp of rémoulade and 1 tsp of chopped bacon on the center of each romaine strip. Top with a fried oyster and wrap the lettuce around the oyster. Pierce the center with a decorated toothpick to secure the oyster.

5. Serve immediately.

Shrimp Toast with Plum Dipping Sauce

My first exposure to shrimp toast wasn't at an Asian restaurant, but at the first catering party I ever worked (as a server/cook). The caterer asked me to prepare a shrimp-toast recipe from one of Martha Stewart's early books, and I ate most of them before she had a chance to serve them to the guests. These take a little work, but they are well worth the effort. For an added bonus, serve both the Plum Dipping Sauce (page 190) and the Pepper-Jelly Dipping Sauce (page 182).

½ lb medium shrimp, peeled and deveined
1 large egg white
¼ cup green onion, minced
1 Tbl cilantro, chopped
⅛ tsp cayenne pepper
½ tsp soy sauce
¼ tsp ginger, freshly chopped
⅛ tsp garlic, minced
¼ tsp Creole seasoning (page 205)
⅛ tsp salt

½ tsp sesame oil
2 large egg yolks
2 Tbl sesame oil
1 Tbl rice vinegar
1 tsp soy sauce
1 Tbl sherry
2 Tbl water
12 slices white bread, crusts removed
6 Tbl vegetable oil
Parsley, for garnish

TIP for Entertaining

For interesting conversation, always devise a diverse guest list.

1. Place the shrimp, egg white, green onion, cilantro, cayenne, ½ tsp soy sauce, ginger, garlic, Creole seasoning, salt, and ½ tsp of the sesame oil in a food processor and pulse 2 or 3 times to finely chop. Do not purée.

2. Put egg yolks, 2 Tbl sesame oil, vinegar, 1 tsp soy sauce, sherry, and water in a shallow bowl and whisk to blend.

3. Spread equal amounts of the shrimp mixture onto slices of bread.

4. Heat 3 Tbl vegetable oil in a large nonstick skillet over medium-high heat. Dip 6 bread slices into egg mixture, coating evenly on both sides. Place them a few at a time, shrimp-side down first, and fry until golden brown, about 4 minutes on each side. Remove from the skillet. Repeat the process with the remaining 3 Tbl vegetable oil and bread slices.

5. Serve with the shrimp side up.

6. Slice each sandwich into 2 triangles, place on a serving plate, and garnish with parsley.

Crab Fritters with Seafood Rémoulade Sauce

Yield: 30-36 fritters

These fritters are easy, quick, and a crowd pleaser.

¾ cup Parmesan cheese, grated
3 eggs
¼ cup parsley, chopped fine
¼ cup green onions, medium dice
¼ cup horseradish
¼ cup sour cream
1½ Tbl garlic, minced
1 Tbl Creole seasoning (page 205)
¼ tsp red pepper, crushed

1 cup flour
½ Tbl hot sauce
10 oz Pepper Jack cheese, grated
6 oz mozzarella cheese, grated
6 oz Cheddar cheese, grated
½ lb lump crabmeat

Oil for frying

1. Place the Parmesan cheese, eggs, parsley, green onions, horseradish, sour cream, garlic, Creole seasoning, red pepper, flour, and hot sauce in an electric mixer and combine at medium speed. Slowly add the 3 cheeses and continue mixing until well blended. Using a spatula, gently fold in the crabmeat by hand.
2. In a fryer or cast-iron skillet, heat 1–1½ quarts of oil to 350 degrees, using a deep-fat thermometer to check the temperature. Drop golf-ball-size spoonfuls of cheese-fritter mixture into hot oil, making sure not to cook too many at once. Cook the fritters for 6–7 minutes, until golden brown.
3. Serve with Seafood Rémoulade Sauce (page 191) for dipping.

Chicken Skewers with Georgia-Peanut Dipping Sauce

Yield: 20 skewers

Make sure to use fish sauce and coconut milk when making the peanut sauce. No substitutes.

SKEWER SOAK
1 cup water
1 Tbl soy sauce
¼ cup coconut milk
20 six-inch wooden skewers

CHICKEN MARINADE
1 lb boneless, skinless chicken breasts,
   cut in 20 strips

¼ cup pineapple juice
2 Tbl soy sauce
1 tsp garlic, minced
1 Tbl sesame oil
¼ cup Thai chili sauce

Peanut oil for frying

1. Combine water, 1 Tbl soy sauce, and coconut milk together and soak the skewers in the mixture for 2–4 hours. Use a plastic-wrapped weight to keep the skewers submerged in the mixture.

2. Thread the chicken onto the soaked skewers, leaving a small portion of the skewer empty so that it can be picked up after cooking.

TIP for Entertaining

Use two parallel skewers instead of one single skewer when grilling. This keeps food from slipping off during cooking and makes it easier to turn.

3. Combine pineapple juice, 2 Tbl soy sauce, garlic, sesame oil, and chili sauce. Pour marinade over the chicken skewers and allow them to soak for 3–4 hours. The chicken should be refrigerated while marinating.

4. Preheat oven to 375 degrees.

5. Over high heat, heat enough peanut oil in a large, nonstick skillet to lightly coat the surface. Drain the marinated skewers. Sear the chicken skewers 6–7 skewers at a time. Flip skewers after 1 or 2 minutes and brown other side. Once both sides are browned, place skewers on a baking sheet. Repeat process with remaining skewers, working in small batches, and adding oil to the pan as needed until all skewers have been seared. Hold until party time.

6. Bake skewers for five to six minutes and serve with Georgia-Peanut Dipping Sauce (page 183).

You may marinate and sear the skewers a day in advance. Wrap and store in the refrigerator until party time. Let skewers sit at room temperature 15 minutes before baking.

Black-and-Blue Nachos

I use filet mignon, but a rib-eye or a New York strip would work well, too.

4 six-inch corn tortillas, each cut into eighths (as you would a pie)
Peanut or vegetable oil, for frying the tortillas

¼ cup milk
¾ cup blue cheese, crumbled
¼ cup Pepper Jack cheese, shredded
1 tsp black pepper, freshly ground

CHEESE MIXTURE
2 tsp olive oil
2 Tbl shallots, minced
2 Tbl yellow onion, minced
1 tsp garlic, minced
½ tsp salt
2 Tbl sun-dried tomatoes, minced
1 tsp dried basil

BLACKENED FILET
½ lb beef tenderloin, cut into 2-inch-long strips, ½ inch in diameter
2 Tbl blackening seasoning
2 tsp kosher salt
2–3 Tbl light olive oil
Parsley, freshly chopped, for garnish

TIP for Entertaining

Always keep a bartender's manual handy, to refer to in the event of an unusual cocktail request.

1. Fry the tortilla chips according to the directions on the package. Season lightly with salt.
2. Place olive oil in a small sauté pan over low heat. Add yellow onion and shallot and cook for 3–4 minutes. Stir in garlic, salt, tomatoes, and basil and cook 2 minutes more. Stir often to prevent the sun-dried tomatoes from burning. Add milk and remove from heat. Allow to cool completely.
3. In a mixing bowl, combine the sundried-tomato/onion mixture with the cheeses. Add pepper.
4. Refrigerate until needed.
5. Dust the strips of beef in the blackening seasoning and sprinkle with kosher salt.
6. Heat olive oil in a cast-iron skillet over high heat. Scatter the beef over the surface of the hot skillet. Turn the meat after 1–2 minutes and cook evenly on all sides. Do not overload the skillet. You may need to cook the beef in batches, depending upon the size of your skillet.
7. The beef can be cooked in advance and held until you are ready to serve the nachos.

TO FINISH

1. Preheat oven to 375 degrees.
2. Place the individual tortilla chips on a large baking sheet.
3. Place 1–2 Tbl of the cheese mixture on the center of each tortilla chip and top with a blackened filet strip. Bake 5 minutes or until cheese is melted.
4. Top with freshly chopped parsley and serve.

Lamb Kebabs with Raspberry-Mint Dipping Sauce

My favorite flavors to accompany lamb are raspberry and mint. This recipe makes good use of them both. When using lesser cuts of lamb, I like to err on the medium side of rare.

SKEWER SOAK

24 skewers

1 cup water

¼ cup lemon juice

¼ cup red wine

LAMB KEBABS

2 lbs leg of lamb, cut into ½-inch cubes

¼ cup lamb rub (page 204)

¼ cup olive oil

1 Tbl kosher salt

Olive oil for frying

1. Combine water, lemon juice, and red wine and soak skewers for 3–4 hours before using.
2. Skewer the lamb onto the soaked skewers, leaving a space at one end so that they can be easily picked up.
3. Season the meat on all sides with lamb rub and refrigerate for 3–4 hours.
4. Preheat oven to 375 degrees.

TIP for Entertaining

When removing food from the grill, always use a clean plate. Never use a plate that has held raw meat. Use tongs to turn meat when grilling; a fork punctures the meat, allowing juices to escape and flavor to be lost.

5. Over high heat, heat enough olive oil to cover the bottom of a large cast-iron skillet. Sprinkle the kabobs with the kosher salt and sear 6 kabobs at a time. Once all kabobs are evenly seared, place on a baking sheet and finish cooking in oven (although, at this point, kabobs can be held in refrigerator for several hours before baking).

6. Bake 5–7 minutes, to medium (or a little longer if the kabobs have been refrigerated).

7. Serve with Raspberry-Mint Dipping Sauce (page 185).

Bloody-Mary Oyster Shooters

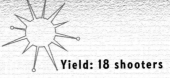

Make a lot, because they're gonna go fast.

18 oysters, freshly shucked

BLOODY MARY COCKTAIL SAUCE
1 cup ketchup
½ cup chili sauce
¼ cup V8 juice
2 Tbl Worcestershire sauce

2 Tbl lemon juice, freshly squeezed
2 Tbl prepared horseradish
1½ Tbl Tabasco sauce
¼ tsp black pepper, freshly ground
½ tsp salt
1 tsp celery salt

1. One day in advance, prepare the cocktail sauce by combining all ingredients except the oysters.
2. To serve, place one oyster in a shot glass, top with 1½ Tbl of the cocktail sauce, and serve.

TIP for Entertaining

Before preparing a recipe, have all of the ingredients measured and ready to be added. This takes the stress out of cooking.

Crabmeat Puffs with Pepper-Jelly Dipping Sauce

Yield: 40-45 puffs

Light and airy, these puffs are a perfect showcase for crabmeat and a perfect pairing with the dipping sauce.

Oil for frying

1 cup flour

½ tsp salt

½ tsp Old Bay seasoning

⅛ tsp black pepper, freshly ground

½ Tbl sugar

½ tsp garlic powder

1½ tsp baking powder

1 egg

1 cup milk

½ lb lump crabmeat

2 Tbl red onion, minced

1. Heat about 1 inch of oil to 325 degrees, using a deep-fat thermometer to check the temperature.
2. In one mixing bowl, blend together all the dry ingredients. In a separate bowl, whisk together the egg and milk. Gently fold the dry ingredients into the milk mixture. Gently fold the crabmeat and red onion into the batter.
3. Drop the mixture into the hot oil 1 Tbl at a time. Fry until the puffs are golden on all sides.
4. Remove and drain on paper towels. If needed, hold the puffs in a 200-degree oven until serving (no longer than 25 minutes).
5. Serve alongside Pepper-Jelly Dipping Sauce (page 182)

Coconut Shrimp with Muscadine Dipping Sauce

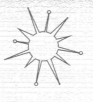

Yield: 24 shrimp

A twist on the old standby from Commander's Palace. If you can't find muscadine jelly in your local market, then you need to move farther south.

24 large (15–20 count) shrimp, peeled, deveined, and butterflied
½ cup cornstarch
¼ tsp kosher salt
¼ tsp black pepper, freshly ground

½ tsp Creole seasoning (page 205)
4 egg whites
2½ cups sweetened shredded coconut, or 2½ cups shredded fresh coconut
Canola or peanut oil, for frying

1. Three-bowl breading procedure: Pat shrimp dry with a paper towel. In the first small bowl combine cornstarch, salt, pepper, and Creole seasoning. In the second bowl, whisk the egg whites until foamy. In the third bowl, place the coconut.
2. Coat the shrimp with the cornstarch mixture and shake off excess. Dip into the egg whites, then press into the coconut, covering entire shrimp. Keep one hand dry to make the process neater.
3. In a large pan, heat about 1 inch of oil to 350 degrees. Check temperature with a deep-fat thermometer. Gently submerge the shrimp, 6 at a time. Fry for approximately 3 minutes or until golden brown.
4. Remove to a rack or paper towel to drain.
5. Serve with Muscadine Dipping Sauce (page 184).

When planning a seated dinner party, always cook for two extra guests. You'll never have to worry about uninvited company, and you'll have leftovers the next day–always a good thing!

TIP for Entertaining

Crawfish-Andouille Hush Puppies

This dish combines a Deep South staple with two Louisiana staples. It's best served with Seafood Rémoulade Sauce (page 191), but Comeback Sauce (page 196) or Creole-Tomato Dipping Sauce (page 186) are good, too. Better still, serve all three.

Oil for frying

1 Tbl plus 1 tsp bacon fat

⅓ cup andouille sausage, finely chopped

½ cup crawfish tails, roughly chopped

½ tsp Creole seasoning (page 205)

1¼ cups yellow cornmeal

½ cup flour

½ tsp salt

1 tsp baking powder

2 eggs, beaten

1 tsp hot sauce

½ cup milk

¼ cup green onion, minced

TIP for Entertaining

Use canola oil for frying. It is low in saturated fat, has a high smoke point, and doesn't detract from the flavor of the food being fried.

1. Using a deep fat thermometer, preheat oil to 325 degrees in a cast-iron skillet, enough to cover approximately 1 inch.
2. In a small sauté pan, heat bacon fat over medium heat.
3. Sauté andouille for 3–4 minutes. Add crawfish and Creole seasoning. Cook 1–2 minutes more, then remove from heat to cool.
4. In a mixing bowl, combine cornmeal, flour, salt, and baking powder. Blend well. In a separate bowl, combine the eggs, hot sauce, milk, onion, and cooled andouille mixture.

   Fold the dry ingredients into the milk mixture and mix until just combined. Do not overmix.
5. Drop the mixture by the tablespoonful into the hot oil and fry for 6–7 minutes until golden brown. Drain on a paper towel and serve with sauce.

Mushroom-Stuffed Pastry

If you're able to find other exotic mushrooms, feel free to substitute your favorites. These freeze well, but make sure to wrap them tightly.

2 Tbl butter
½ lb fresh mushrooms—button, portobello, and shiitake recommended
½ cup onion, minced
¼ cup shallots, minced
1 tsp garlic, minced
1 tsp poultry seasoning (page 207)
½ tsp salt

⅛ tsp black pepper, freshly ground
1 tsp fresh thyme, chopped
½ tsp fresh rosemary, chopped
¼ cup port wine
¼ cup goat cheese
1 Tbl parsley, freshly chopped
1 recipe Easy Pastry (page 208)

1. In a large skillet, melt the butter over medium-high heat. Sauté mushrooms, onion, shallot, garlic, poultry seasoning, and salt for 6–7 minutes. Add the black pepper, thyme, rosemary, and port wine, cooking until all liquid has evaporated. Remove from the heat and blend in the goat cheese and parsley. Cool mixture completely.

2. Roll out the prepared pastry to a ⅛-inch thickness.

TIP for Entertaining

During the hectic holidays, the best type of party to give is a "come and go" open house, which enables you to spend more time with each guest.

3. Using a round cookie cutter, cut dough into 2½-inch circles. Place 1–1½ tsp of filling onto center of the dough circle. Using fingers, pinch the edges in an upward direction, forming a small, half-moon-shaped tartlet. Place on baking sheet and freeze. (These must be cooked from a frozen state.)

4. If preparing well in advance, the pastries can be placed in a plastic bag once frozen and held for 1–2 months in the freezer.

5. To bake, preheat the oven to 350 degrees. Bake for 12–15 minutes, until pastry is golden brown. Serve warm or at room temperature.

Miniature Grilled Pimento-Cheese Sandwiches

You'd better make a bunch of them. They also freeze well.

1 large loaf sliced white bread, crusts
   removed
1 recipe Pâté of the South (page 132)
1-1½ cups salted butter, softened

1. Preheat oven to 375 degrees.
2. Bring pimento cheese to room temperature, making it easy to spread. Divide pimento cheese evenly among half of the bread slices (approximately 9–10 slices).
3. Spread evenly on bread slices and top with remaining bread. Spread a thin layer of the softened butter onto both sides of the sandwiches.
4. Heat a large nonstick skillet or an electric griddle to medium heat. Brown both sides of sandwiches. Remove sandwiches from heat and cut in half on the diagonal, creating 2 small, triangular-shaped sandwiches. Place on a lined baking sheet. Bake 4 minutes. Serve hot.

TIP for Entertaining

Place finger sandwiches and canapés in a shallow container, cover with a damp cloth, and refrigerate for up to eight hours before a party.

To make rolled sandwiches, the ingredients should always be ground or chopped finely. The bread can be rolled with a rolling pin, too.

26

The History of the Party, According to Robert

My earliest memory is of a cocktail party my parents were hosting in the living room of our small home on Twenty-second Avenue in Hattiesburg, Mississippi.

The year was 1965, and I was four years old. After a steady Saturday evening diet of *Flipper*, *I Dream of Jeannie*, and *Get Smart*, I was under the covers at 8:30 P.M. I can remember lying in my bed, fully awake, hearing the strange, magical sounds coming from the living room—the clinking of ice in glasses, laughter, excited conversation, background music, and dancing—the quiet roar of a smoky room in full bloom. It was romantic, it was mysterious, and it sounded like fun.

It was a cocktail party smack-dab in the middle of the "Cocktail Era." In the living room, Dean Martin and Nat King Cole were crooning on the hi-fi system—a piece of wooden furniture as large as a sideboard. In the dining room, a small mahogany dining table was lined with cocktail weenies, meatballs, cheese spreads, and sour cream–laced cold dips. Scattered around both rooms were bowlfuls of salted peanuts, plates filled with my grandmother's bacon-wrapped crackers, and ashtrays of all shapes, sizes, and colors. The kitchen doubled as a bar and a well-stocked cabinet full of scotch, bourbon, vodka, gin, soda, and tonic was open all night. Throughout the house were cigarettes.

Parties were full of cigarettes. The world was full of cigarettes. People smoked on television, they smoked while cooking, they smoked while eating, they smoked while drinking, they smoked while driving, they smoked while drinking and driving, they smoked during sex, they smoked after sex, they smoked while sleeping, and they smoked while smoking. The Camel ads of the day claimed, "More doctors smoke Camel than any other cigarette." Old Gold promised, "Not a cough in a carload." Today, smoking is taboo, and during a party is mostly reserved for the backyard, carport, sidewalk, or balcony. But in those days, smoking was sexy.

I was conceived on New Year's Eve, 1960, before cigarettes and scotch were replaced by Lamaze and sonograms. Parties are in my genetic makeup. I have a photograph of my mother, six months pregnant with me, at a Fourth of July cocktail party, a double scotch on the rocks in one hand, a Benson & Hedges 100 in the other, leaning back in a chair, midlaugh, a good time being had by all. I have always loved a party; I was born into it.

In those days, there was a party around every corner, and the basics of the Southern cocktail party were: French-onion soup dips, melted processed-cheese dips with canned tomatoes, and cocktail weenies swimming in vats of bottled barbecue sauce. Frill picks were used by the upper crust, and meatballs were only brought out during special occasions.

In the summertime on the Gulf Coast, we entertained guests with boiled shrimp, boiled crawfish, and crab salad on crackers. There were, of course, bowls of salted peanuts, glasses full of vodka and gin, and plenty of cigarettes.

In my high school years, a party consisted of a keg of beer near a wooded lake, accompanied by a microwaved burrito from the 7-Eleven and a bottle of Visine.

High school dances always held "breakfasts" afterward, but most couples didn't show up—and when they did, no one ate. My college years took the party inside with more kegs, trash cans full of grain-alcohol punch, hazy memories, and smoke-filled late nights at the Waffle House.

The South Mississippi bachelor special was a football game on the television and a plate of microwaved deer sausage with a side of French's mustard, not a frill pick in sight. Not being one who hunts deer, or one who kept deer sausage in the refrigerator, I usually opted for chips and salsa.

Mardi Gras parties were the only respite from the boring and uninventive party menus of the 1960s and '70s. Although I live in what would be considered one of the notches in the Bible Belt, we celebrated Mardi Gras with abandon and partied as hard as any of our neighbors ninety miles south of us. During Mardi Gras, the food improved and the wine flowed. There were grillades and grits, French-inspired egg dishes, seafood-brunch specialties, king cakes, and plenty of milk punch, bloody Marys, mimosas, and cigarettes.

Early in my married life, parties began to turn. I was full-bore into my restaurant career, and catering came easy. New foodstuffs were hitting the local markets. Processed cheese gave way to goat cheese. Fresh herbs were available at the corner grocer. Cans of tuna were tossed out in favor of fresh-caught Gulf of Mexico tuna, the yellowfin variety, served raw. There were oyster shooters and sides of salmon, pâtés, terrines, and caviar-laced canapés. Parties gained a whole new air—a fresher air—as the cigarettes fell victim to class-action lawsuits and effective counter-advertising.

I love to entertain. Sharing food with friends is one of life's greatest pleasures. Entertaining should be easy and fun. Items should be prepared well in advance, so the host can enjoy the party, too. The freezer should be filled with enough emergency entertaining provisions that when a guest or a group of guests drop in, food is not a problem.

It is telling that my earliest memory is not of a toy, or a relative, or a favorite blanket, but a party. Today, I have given up drinking and smoking. I got married—which almost forced me to give up sex—and now my only vice is food. But as long as family, food, friends, and a party are around the corner, I'm just fine.

On the Sideboard

Yellowfin Tuna Tartare with Avocado Relish and Wonton Chips

Black-Eyed-Pea Cakes with Roasted Red-Pepper Aioli

Fried Garlic and Goat-Cheese Grits with Blackberry-Tasso Chutney

Tasso and Smoked-Cheddar Savory Cheesecake

Miniature Shrimp and Grits

Shrimp Tarts with Dirty-Rice Pie Crust

Parmigiano-Reggiano-Crusted Asparagus

Marinated and Roasted Vegetables

Artichoke Tarts

Crab Cakes with Lemon-Caper Tartar Sauce

Smoked Beef Tenderloin with Chive-and-Tarragon Sauce and Horseradish Mustard

Baked Stuffed Brie

Barbara Jane's Tomato Sandwiches

The World's Last Deviled Egg

Marinated Crab Claws

Yellowfin Tuna Tartare with Avocado Relish and Wonton Chips

The ingredients must be fresh. Do not substitute; you won't be sorry. This dish is a true crowd-pleaser with a lot of "wow" appeal.

¼ cup green onion, minced

1 tsp fresh ginger, minced

2 Tbl cilantro, chopped

2 Tbl toasted sesame seeds

1 Tbl sesame oil

1 tsp fish sauce

½ tsp hot sauce

2 Tbl soy sauce

1 tsp honey

1 tsp sherry

1 tsp rice vinegar

2 Tbl cottonseed oil

½ pound fresh yellowfin tuna, small dice

AVOCADO RELISH

1 Tbl fresh lime juice

1 tsp cottonseed oil (or canola oil)

1 tsp sesame-seed oil

¼ tsp garlic, minced

1 Tbl red onion, small dice

1 tsp parsley, freshly chopped

2 tsp red bell pepper, small dice

1 medium-sized ripe avocado

¼ tsp salt

⅛ tsp cayenne pepper

5 sheets fresh egg-roll wrappers to make wonton crackers

TIP for Entertaining

Prepare three to four appetizer portions per person for pre-dinner cocktails, and six pieces per person for a cocktail party.

Low on serving trays? Cover a baking pan with multicolored napkins or an elegant fabric.

1. To make the Tuna Tartare: Combine all ingredients except for yellowfin tuna and blend well. (The diced tuna should be added to the sesame-seed mixture just before serving.)

2. Combine first 7 ingredients of avocado relish and blend well. Quickly fold in the avocado. If making in advance, place the pit in the relish and press plastic wrap directly onto the relish, sealing it off from any air exposure. Add salt and cayenne peppers. Refrigerate.

3. Using a cookie cutter, cut 2½-inch circles into the center of egg-roll wrappers. Fry according to package directions.

4. To serve, place 1½ tsp of the Tuna Tartare mixture and 1 tsp avocado relish on the wonton crackers.

Black-Eyed Pea Cakes with Roasted Red Pepper Aioli

Yield: 20 cakes

This pure Southern treat with a twist is a perfect use for leftover black-eyed peas. However, the recipe is so good, you'll end up making them exclusively for this purpose and using the leftover black-eyed peas for a side dish with supper.

1 Tbl bacon grease or canola oil

¼ cup red onion, small dice

½ cup green onion, thinly sliced

¼ cup red bell pepper, small dice

½ tsp garlic, minced

2 tsp cumin

¼ tsp Creole seasoning (page 205)

½ tsp salt

3 cups black-eyed peas, cooked

¾ cup panko bread crumbs

2 eggs

¼ cup olive oil

¼ cup sour cream

¼ cup roasted red peppers, small dice

Olive oil for frying

1. Melt the bacon grease over medium heat and cook onions, bell pepper, garlic, and seasonings for 4–5 minutes. Remove from heat.

2. Place 2 cups of the black-eyed peas with the eggs into a food processor, and purée until smooth.

TIP for Entertaining

Substitute crème fraîche in recipes that call for sour cream. It has fewer preservatives, tastes better, and doesn't curdle.

3. Remove from processor and place processed peas in a separate bowl. Add vegetables, panko, and remaining cup of whole peas, stirring gently. Firmly form the mixture into 1-oz cakes and refrigerate for 1 hour.

4. Preheat oven to 300 degrees.

5. In a large nonstick sauté pan, heat 1–2 Tbl of olive oil over medium-high heat. Gently place the cakes into hot pan and brown on both sides. Add more oil as needed.

Once all cakes are brown, place on a lightly oiled baking sheet, and bake 10 minutes.

6. Top each black-eyed-pea cake with a small dollop of sour cream and a few pieces of diced roasted peppers.

Fried Garlic and Goat-Cheese Grits with Blackberry-Tasso Chutney

Yield: Feeds 10-12 people

The only way to make grits more Southern is to deep-fry them. Take your time when breading the grits so that they don't break down in the hot oil. The blackberry chutney has multiple uses in other dishes.

1 Tbl butter	1 tsp hot sauce
1½ tsp garlic, minced	3 oz goat cheese
1 tsp Creole seasoning (page 205)	Oil for frying
1 tsp salt	1 cup seasoned flour (page 208)
½ tsp black pepper, freshly ground	1 cup egg wash (3 eggs beaten with ¼
3 cups milk	cup cream)
1 cup grits	1 cup bread crumbs

1. In a 1½-quart sauce pot, melt butter over low heat, and cook the garlic with Creole seasoning, salt, and pepper for five minutes. Do not brown the garlic.
2. Add the milk and bring to a slow simmer. Add the grits, stirring constantly. Cook for 15 minutes, stirring often to prevent grits from forming lumps or sticking.

TIP for Entertaining

Keep prep stress at a minimum; serve what you know, and never experiment with first-time dishes when guests are involved.

3. Remove grits from heat and blend in the goat cheese and hot sauce. Immediately pour the grits into an 8 x 8-inch baking dish. Refrigerate overnight.

4. Using a deep-fat thermometer preheat approximately 1 inch of oil to 325 degrees in a cast-iron skillet.

5. To make the grits cakes for frying, cut the chilled grits into 8 squares. Then cut the squares in half diagonally, forming a triangle.

6. Three-bowl breading procedure: Place seasoned flour in the first bowl, egg wash in the second, and bread crumbs in the third.

7. Dredge grits cakes in the flour, shaking off excess. Dip into egg wash, then into bread crumb mixture. Coat grits thoroughly.

8. Fry in small batches until golden and drain onto paper towels.

9. Top with Blackberry-Tasso Chutney (page 199) and serve hot.

Tasso and Smoked-Cheddar Savory Cheesecake

Yield: 10-12 slices

One of the best-tasting, and most versatile, recipes in this book, this dish can be made four or five days in advance. It's beautiful on a sideboard for a cocktail party, perfect with a salad for lunch, and an excellent side item with an entrée for dinner. Country ham, chopped bacon, or cooked sausage can be substituted for the tasso (Cajun-spiced ham).

CRUST
2 cups panko bread crumbs
1 cup Parmesan cheese
1 Tbl fresh thyme
1 Tbl parsley
½ cup melted butter
1 tsp black pepper, freshly ground

FILLING
1 Tbl butter
1½ cup tasso, medium dice
½ cup onion, minced
1 Tbl garlic, minced

½ pound cream cheese, softened
½ pound smoked Cheddar cheese, finely grated
3 eggs plus 2 yolks
¼ cup sour cream
½ tsp salt
1 tsp Creole seasoning (page 205)
¼ tsp black pepper
¼ tsp cayenne pepper
1 Tbl Worcestershire sauce
½ cup green onions, chopped
2 Tbl red bell peppers, finely chopped

1. Preheat oven to 275 degrees.
2. Combine all the ingredients for the crust.
3. Press into a 9–10-inch springform pan, covering the bottom completely and bringing the crust 1½ inches up the sides. Bake crust 5 minutes and allow to cool.
4. In a medium-sized sauté pan, melt the butter and cook the tasso, onion, and garlic for 3–4 minutes. Allow to cool.

5. While tasso mixture is cooling, beat the cheeses together until soft in a mixing bowl. Add eggs, one at a time, allowing them to incorporate. Add remaining ingredients, then add the cooled tasso mixture.

6. Pour the filling into the par-baked crust and bake 45–60 minutes.

7. Let the cheesecake cool completely before cutting. Dip a clean knife into hot water to cut, wiping knife clean, and re-dipping into water after every slice.

8. Can be made two days in advance. Remove from refrigerator 1–2 hours before serving.

Old Bay seasoning is perfect for seasoning shrimp.

TIP for Entertaining

Miniature Shrimp and Grits

Shrimp and grits became popular in Southern restaurants in the late 1980s. This is a preparation that allows them to be handheld. Clarified butter is butter that has been heated and solids removed.

¼ cup quick grits
1 cup heavy cream
1 tsp salt
1 tsp Creole seasoning (page 205)

20 large shrimp, peeled and split in half lengthwise
1 tsp cracked black peppercorns
¾ cup BBQ Shrimp Stock (below)

GRITS BISCUITS
1½ cups flour
1 Tbl sugar
2 tsp baking soda
1 tsp baking powder
2 tsp salt
1 tsp black pepper, freshly ground
¼ cup shortening
1 egg
½ cup buttermilk
1 recipe grits

BBQ SHRIMP STOCK *(Yield: 2 cups)*
½ cups white wine
1 cup shrimp stock (tips page 45)
2 Tbl Creole seasoning (page 205)
1½ Tbl Worcestershire sauce
1½ Tbl lemon juice
3 tsp paprika
2 tsp garlic, minced
2 tsp liquid crab boil
2 Tbl Creole mustard
1 bay leaf
1 tsp hot sauce

BBQ SHRIMP
2 Tbl clarified butter

1. Combine grits, cream, and Creole seasoning in a small covered baking dish and cook in a 300-degree oven for 45 minutes. Remove and cool slightly.
2. Combine all dry ingredients, then, using a fork, blend the shortening into the dry mixture.

3. Whip together the egg, buttermilk, and grits. Fold the wet ingredients into the dry ingredients and blend well. Do not overmix.

4. Roll out biscuits to ½-inch thickness and cut out 2-inch circles.

5. Bake at 375 degrees for 18 minutes.

6. Bring all ingredients to a boil, immediately remove from heat, and cool (this can be done 2–3 days ahead of time).

7. Melt clarified butter in a skillet and add shrimp. Sauté for two minutes. Add cracked black peppercorns and BBQ Shrimp Stock and cook until shrimp are just done. Make sure the cold BBQ Shrimp Stock is stirred vigorously before adding to skillet.

8. Top each biscuit with one piece of the BBQ Shrimp and serve.

Shrimp stock is a fast and flavorful substitute for meat stock. Simply simmer fresh shrimp shells, a few slices of onion, and a half of a celery stalk in enough water to cover.

TIP for Entertaining

Shrimp Tarts with Dirty-Rice Pie Crust

Yield: 10-12 servings

The crust takes a little work, though it's worth every minute spent preparing it. A perfect use for leftover dirty rice. The crust also freezes well, so make extra.

1 Tbl butter
¼ cup onion, minced
½ lb shrimp, cleaned
1 tsp Old Bay seasoning
¼ tsp black pepper
¼ tsp salt
1 tsp garlic, minced
¼ cup white wine
¼ cup cream cheese, softened
¼ cup Parmesan cheese, grated
1 egg
2 Tbl sour cream
1 tsp Creole seasoning (page 205)

⅛ tsp cayenne pepper
2 tsp Worcestershire sauce
2 tsp red bell pepper, finely chopped
2 Tbl green onion, chopped

DIRTY-RICE CRUST
2½ cups flour
½ cup shortening
¼ tsp salt
¾ cup dirty rice, cooked (page 210)
1 egg
¼ cup buttermilk

1. Heat butter over medium heat in a large sauté pan. Add onion, shrimp, Old Bay, black pepper, and salt and sauté until shrimp are thoroughly cooked. Add garlic and white wine, and cook until the wine has completely evaporated. Remove from the heat and cool completely.
2. Place all ingredients, except the shrimp mixture, bell peppers, and green onion, into a food processor and purée until smooth. Add the shrimp mixture and pulse to roughly chop the shrimp. Gently fold in the bell peppers and green onion by hand, scraping sides of bowl.

3. For the crust: Preheat the oven to 350 degrees. Blend the first 3 ingredients together with a pastry-cutter or a fork. Add the rice, and blend once more. Beat the egg and buttermilk together. Slowly add egg mixture to flour mixture, 1 Tbl at a time, until pie dough becomes moist and forms a ball. Wrap and refrigerate 1 hour before rolling. Roll out on a floured surface (if dough is stiff and very cold, let stand until dough is cool but malleable).

4. Roll out crust into a rectangular shape (approximately 18 x 12 inches). The dough should be ⅛-inch thick. Cut dough into 3-inch squares. Place 1 Tbl of filling onto the center of each square. Fold the 4 corners into the center of the filling and pinch corners together.

5. Place on an ungreased baking sheet and refrigerate for 30 minutes. Bake for 15–18 minutes.

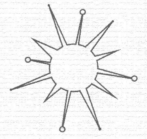

Parmigiano-Reggiano-Crusted Asparagus

1 bunch asparagus, medium-sized, ends removed (18-20 spears)

1 package phyllo dough sheets, thawed

½ lb butter, melted

1 cup Parmigiano Reggiano cheese, freshly grated

1 tsp black pepper, freshly ground

2 egg whites, well beaten

1. Preheat oven to 375 degrees.
2. Bring 1 qt of lightly salted water to a boil.
3. Cook the asparagus for 1 minute, then drain immediately.
4. Place one sheet of the phyllo dough on a flat surface, brush with melted butter, and sprinkle with 1 tsp cheese. Top with another layer of phyllo dough, and repeat the process. Sprinkle with a pinch of black pepper. Cut the sheet in half, so that the two halves are each the length of the asparagus. Place an asparagus spear at one end of a dough sheet, and tightly roll the dough around the asparagus. Repeat the process.
5. Place the rolls on a lined baking sheet, leaving room between them. Repeat this process until all asparagus has been wrapped. You may have leftover phyllo; if so, wrap it well and refreeze.
6. Using a pastry brush, lightly coat the outsides of the rolls with the egg white. Sprinkle any remaining cheese on the roll.
7. Bake for 15–20 minutes, until the rolls are golden brown.

Marinated and Roasted Vegetables

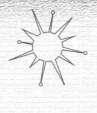

Yield: 12-14 servings

This dish makes a beautiful statement on any sideboard. Sprinkle a few tablespoons of freshly grated Parmigiano Reggiano over the top just before serving. Serve alongside grilled artichoke hearts.

1 large zucchini, cut into ½-inch disks

1 large summer squash, cut into ½-inch disks

1 bunch asparagus, trimmed

1 large red bell pepper, cut into ½-inch circles

1 small red onion, cut into ½-inch circles

2 portobello mushrooms, stems removed and gills scraped from underside

1 small eggplant, peeled and cut into ½-inch circles

MARINADE

1 Tbl Creole mustard

¼ cup balsamic vinegar

2 tsp salt

1 tsp black pepper

2 tsp garlic, minced

1 tsp fresh thyme

1 Tbl fresh basil

1 cup olive oil

1. Preheat oven to 400 degrees.

2. Combine all the marinade ingredients and stir vigorously.

3. Then, in a large stainless-steel bowl, toss all of the vegetables with the marinade and refrigerate 30 minutes.

4. Drain vegetables and reserve excess marinade. Arrange vegetables in a single layer on baking sheets. Roast vegetables for 15 minutes. Cool before serving.

Artichoke Tarts

This can also be served as a side dish with dinner. It can be made two days in advance and refrigerated. To serve it after it has been refrigerated, allow it to sit at room temperature for one hour before serving.

2 six-ounce jars marinated artichoke
  hearts
1 cup yellow onion, minced
¼ cup red bell pepper, small dice
1 Tbl garlic, minced
⅛ tsp oregano
⅛ tsp thyme
4 eggs

1 tsp Creole mustard
1 tsp Creole seasoning (page 205)
½ cup panko bread crumbs
¼ tsp hot sauce
½ cup Parmesan cheese, grated
1 cup Cheddar cheese, grated
1 tsp black pepper, freshly ground
¼ cup green onion, minced

1. Preheat oven to 325 degrees.
2. Drain artichokes, reserving 2 Tbl of the marinating liquid.
3. Place the 2 Tbl of liquid in a small sauté pan over medium heat. Add onion and red pepper and cook 3–4 minutes. Add the garlic, oregano, and thyme and cook 2–3 minutes more. Remove from heat and cool.
4. Roughly chop the artichokes. Whip the eggs and mix all the ingredients together in a mixing bowl.
5. Spread the mixture into a 9-inch buttered pie pan. Bake 30 minutes.
6. Remove from oven and cool to room temperature. Cut into 16 or 8 wedges and serve.

The most important rule of entertaining is to make your guests feel welcome.

TIP for
Entertaining

Crab Cakes with Lemon-Caper Tartar Sauce

Yield: 18-20 crab cakes

My rules for crabmeat: Buy fresh. Buy the best, and treat it sweet. Be gentle with crabmeat to keep the lobes as large as possible. Seafood Rémoulade Sauce (page 191) would be a nice alternative to the Lemon-Caper Tartar Sauce (page 187).

¼ cup parsley, chopped

2 tsp hot sauce

1 tsp salt

3 eggs plus 3 egg yolks

¾ cup homemade mayonnaise (page 193) or top-quality store-bought

¾ cup sour cream

1 Tbl Creole seasoning (page 205)

1 tsp fresh lemon zest

1 tsp Old Bay seasoning

1½ pounds lump crabmeat

1½ cups saltine crackers, crumbled

1 stick butter

1. Mix together all the ingredients except the crabmeat, cracker crumbs, and butter. Gently add the crabmeat. Add ½ cup of the cracker crumbs, folding in until just incorporated. Form into 2½-oz cakes. Use the remaining cracker crumbs to bread the outside of the crab cakes. Place in refrigerator for 45 minutes before cooking.

2. In a large nonstick pan, melt butter over medium heat. Place crab cakes in hot pan, leaving room so they can easily be turned. Brown on each side and place on baking sheet until ready to serve.

3. Finish the crab cakes in a 350-degree preheated oven for 8–10 minutes.

Buy food in season. Never buy cheap or generic supplies; quality will always win out.

TIP for Entertaining

Smoked Beef Tenderloin with Chive-and-Tarragon Sauce and Horseradish Mustard

Yield: 16-20 servings

This is always one of the first items to go, so make enough for everyone. Experiment with different varieties of wood chips for different flavors. If your smoker or barbecue does not maintain a consistent temperature, the beef tenderloin can be transferred to a roasting pan and finished in a 200-degree oven. The sauces work great with sandwiches, too. Keep them stored in the fridge throughout the year.

1 beef tenderloin, cleaned and trimmed
   (approx. 4-5 pounds)
2 Tbl steak seasoning (page 206)
2 cups hickory chips

1. Soak hickory chips for 1 hour prior to smoking.
2. Prepare a smoker to a constant 225–250 degrees. Drain wood chips and place half over the lit charcoal.
3. Place the beef tenderloin in the smoker. After 30 minutes, add remaining hickory chips to the charcoal. Continue cooking until desired level of doneness is reached (in a 200-degree smoker, it will take approximately 1 hour to reach medium).
4. Serve warm, cold, or at room temperature with Chive-and-Tarragon Sauce (page 188) and Horseradish Mustard (page 194).

Baked Stuffed Brie

Make sure to carefully seal the Brie in the pastry so the cheese doesn't ooze out when baking. Bake straight from the refrigerator; do not let the pastry sit out before baking. Apples can be substituted for pears.

1 16-oz wheel Brie
1 pie crust
2 Tbl butter
¼ cup shallots, minced
1½ cups fresh pears, small dice
¼ cup Calvados or brandy

1 tsp pepper, freshly ground
2 tsp thyme, freshly chopped
½ cup almond slivers, toasted and
    chopped
Egg wash (1 egg, 2 Tbl water)

1. In a medium-sized skillet, melt the butter over medium heat. Cook the shallots for 2 minutes. Add the diced pears. Cook pears for 5 minutes. Add the Calvados and simmer until almost dry. Stir in the pepper, thyme, and chopped almonds. Remove mixture from the heat, and cool completely before stuffing Brie.

2. To prepare the Brie, use a spoon to scrape the rind off of the cheese. Dip a sharp knife into hot water and slice the cheese round across the center, cutting in half horizontally so that you have two thin disks or wedges. Place the pear mixture on top of one of the half-wheels of cheese (spreading on exposed-cheese side), and top with the remaining half-wheel of cheese.

3. Roll the pie crust to ⅛-inch thickness and wrap Brie in pastry. Make sure Brie is entirely enclosed in pastry. Place—seam side down—on a baking sheet and brush with egg wash.

4. Refrigerate for 30 minutes before cooking.

5. Bake in a 350-degree oven for 40 minutes.

6. Remove from oven and allow pastry to cool for 10 minutes before serving.

Barbara Jane's Tomato Sandwiches

Yield: 50-60 sandwiches

The first time I ate these, my friend Barbara Jane Foote used Roma tomatoes that had been picked from her garden just hours earlier. There are many versions of this Southern party staple. Hers is the best. As always, use garden-fresh tomatoes for the best results.

2 cups homemade mayonnaise (page 193) or top quality store-bought

½ cup sour cream

2 Tbl bacon grease, reserved from cooked bacon

6 green onion, minced

1 twelve-ounce package Wright's thick-sliced bacon, cooked, finely chopped

1 package (2 loaves) Pepperidge Farm Hot & Crusty bread

5–6 Roma tomatoes, sliced (8–10 slices per tomato, depending on size)

Salt and pepper, to taste

Fresh parsley or basil, finely chopped

TIP for Entertaining

To peel tomatoes, bring a pot of water to boil, add tomatoes, and boil fifteen seconds. Drain and rinse them in cold water. The skins will come right off.

1. Combine mayonnaise, sour cream, bacon grease, onions, and chopped bacon, and stir well.
2. Slice bread into 25–30 rounds per loaf. Spread mayonnaise onto bread rounds, top with a tomato slice, and sprinkle with salt and pepper. Sprinkle lightly with parsley or basil just before serving.

Note: These can be made a day ahead. Arrange sandwiches on a cookie sheet in a single layer and cover well with plastic wrap. Refrigerate. If holding, wait to season sandwiches with salt and pepper, and parsley or basil, until just before serving.

The World's Last Deviled Egg

I have to make a batch for the guests and a separate batch for my kids. They love them.

1 dozen eggs, hard boiled, peeled and cut
   in half, lengthwise
2 tsp white balsamic vinegar
⅓ cup homemade mayonnaise (page
   193) or top quality store-bought
¼ cup sour cream
1 Tbl pickle relish

1½ tsp salt
1 Tbl Creole mustard
2 tsp yellow mustard
⅛ tsp white pepper
⅛ tsp garlic powder
Paprika and fresh parsley to garnish
   (optional)

1. Remove the yolks from the hard-boiled eggs and place them in a mixing bowl. Add the rest of the ingredients and beat with an electric mixer until smooth. Use a pastry bag to fill the egg whites with the yolk mixture. Sprinkle with the paprika and fresh parsley.

TIP for Entertaining

To peel hard-boiled eggs, gently crack the eggs in a few places and drop them into a bowl of cold water. Let them rest for at least thirty minutes. When removed, the shells will drop right off.

Marinated Crab Claws

These must be prepared no earlier than one day in advance and no later than six hours before the party. That's an eighteen-hour window, for those who don't want to do the math.

1 cup extra-virgin olive oil	1 Tbl Worcestershire sauce
¼ cup white balsamic vinegar	½ tsp dry oregano
2 Tbl lemon juice	¼ cup pickled okra, chopped
½ cup green onion, chopped	1 Tbl jalapeños, minced
2 Tbl red onion, minced	1 tsp salt
2 Tbl celery, finely chopped	½ tsp black pepper, freshly ground
2 Tbl fresh chives, chopped	1 tsp hot sauce
1 Tbl parsley, chopped	1 lb blue crab claws
1 tsp garlic, minced	

1. In a large glass bowl, combine all the ingredients except the claws. Whisk to mix well. Add crab claws and toss to coat. Cover and refrigerate at least 6 hours or overnight.
2. Serve chilled.

Always use a fork when handling habanero chilies. Always wash your hands, the cutting board, and the knife and fork with soap and water afterward. Never rub your eyes while preparing chilies.

TIP for Entertaining

The Invasion of the Whores de Orvrays

T hey're gonna have Mexican prostitutes there," said Forrest.

"How do you know?" I said.

"I heard Mrs. Wagner on the telephone. They're bringing them in from some town south of the border. Mexico, probably. A town called Orvrays, I think it was."

"That's not necessarily in Mexico," said Chris. "Orvrays could be any Latin American country." Chris was our intellectual. His father was a college professor.

So began the most memorable episode of the summer of 1972—my sixth-grade year—the two-week period our entire neighborhood spent in anticipation of busloads of lovesick floozies invading our town from somewhere south of the border.

The eavesdropee, Mrs. Wagner, was a native of Hungary. It was said that she came from the same town from which the Gabor sisters hailed. Even though she had lived in South Mississippi for eighteen years, her accent was thick and awkward. She pronounced "with" as "weet" and "the" as "dee" and had an affinity for goulash and paprika. Accent or not, there was no mistaking the word "whores." It was the world's oldest profession and along with it, the world's oldest pronunciation. There was no doubt in anyone's mind that Mrs. Wagner was talking about exotic and lustful Latin ladies, and that they were probably en route to our town at that exact minute.

It was widely understood that Mrs. Wagner, being European, had a different sensibility than the other mothers in the neighborhood. "She's more open-minded," Chris said. "She has a laissez-faire attitude."

"You mean she likes girls?"

"No. She's liberal. And she asked who was bringing the whores de Orvrays. I heard it. She said '*de*,' but my sister said that '*de*' means '*of*' in Spanish. They're whores of Orvrays, Mexico, and they're coming to the Johnsons' party. Just think, Mexican hookers in our neighborhood."

"I wonder if Hugh Hefner will be there, too," I said.

"Are you sure she didn't say Norway?"

"Nope, she said Orvrays, and they'll be here in two weeks."

The news spread from brother to brother, brother to sister, sister to mother, mother to father, and within a matter of hours word of the Johnsons' upcoming party had traveled to the outermost reaches of the Hillendale subdivision.

For the next two weeks, every woman in a twelve-block radius had a telephone cocked and loaded between her shoulder and ear; fathers were meeting each other in backyards; bridge clubs were abuzz; and beauty parlors were rife with scandalous scuttlebutt. All were covering the same subject: the painted ladies that were coming to the Johnsons' party. The Bible-Belt gossip line in our small Southern town was on all-out full-bore ringing-off-the-hook red alert.

In a town where the local district attorney had banned *Last Tango in Paris* from being shown in local theaters, a busload of ladies of the evening was a noteworthy event. At the grocery store, at the ballpark, and at church—male, female, young and old, everyone was talking about the upcoming Johnson party.

Three days before the party, Mildred Baker passed away while sitting in the dryer chair at Marilyn's Beauty Parlor. She had gone under the dome around 8:30 A.M., had a massive coronary, then sat—stiff and unattended, beehive baking—until closing time, when the nail girl realized Mildred "hadn't moved in a while." The coroner was never able to pinpoint the exact time of death, due to Mildred's elongated exposure to the heat of the dryer, but most believe she passed sometime around 9:30 A.M., after Celia Rhodes and Betty Chapel came in talking about the Johnson party.

The men of the neighborhood were uncharacteristically low-key. There was a different air about them—a flicker of hope. Some publicly disparaged Mr. Johnson; some secretly wished they could trade places.

The event was turning out to be more scandalous than the Franklin Christmas Tree Controversy six months earlier. The Franklin family was from "somewhere up north," my mother used to say. I later found out that they were from Kentucky . . . a Northern state, to most in the area. On their first Christmas in town, the Franklins had committed the cardinal Yuletide sin: blue lights on a metallic silver Christmas tree. My mother wrote it off as the act of Catholics, others blamed the Franklins' Northern breeding, but most chalked it up to a lack of good taste.

Like the Franklins, the upcoming party's host, Dick Johnson, was an interloper. He had arrived two summers prior, after being hired as the new marketing manager at one of the town's banks. "Marketing," my mother said. "He's probably from New York." He and his two sons moved into the old Tyler home two blocks from my house. The Tylers had moved out after getting the first divorce ever granted in Forrest County, Mississippi—an event, as it turned out, even more scandalous than a silver-and-blue Christmas tree.

Mr. Johnson was a Jack Cassidy look-alike who sported tiny Speedo bathing suits around the country-club swimming pool, kept *Playboy* on his bedside table, and wore a goatee. His teenage sons tortured cats and shot at neighborhood kids with BB guns. Over the years, there had been rampant stories of wild "key parties," skinny-dipping, swinging, and all manner of sinful and hedonistic debauchery at the Johnsons'. Certainly a party with exotic Latin ladies of the evening shipped in from Mexico wouldn't be a stretch.

The Johnson party was a turning point in our adolescence. Until then, the highlight of our hot Mississippi summers had been prank-calling neighbors on the telephone, the main victims being the family of a college professor named Dr. Orange. "Is Dr. Apple there?" we would ask, stifling giggles. "I'm sorry, you've got the wrong fruit," an Orange on the other end would reply. It was always good for a laugh, and I think for at least the first two hundred times, the Orange family got a kick out of it, too.

On the day of the party, we awoke early. Our entire day was spent in the neighborhood tree house across the street from the Johnsons'. We wanted to see the whores from Orvrays arrive, watch them pile out of the limousine and sashay half-dressed into the house. The music would then be turned up, the lights would be turned down, and all manner of sexual depravity would ensue.

As night fell, teenagers looking for action, frat boys in search of cheap thrills, and most of the uninvited men of the neighborhood loaded into jeeps, vans, and station wagons and cruised up and down the street trying to catch a glimpse of a real, live hooker. At 7:30 P.M. guests had begun arriving and there wasn't a whore in sight.

Had we not gotten out of bed early enough? Had we missed the floozies' arrival the night before? Did Mr. Johnson smuggle them into the house in the catering van? At 9:15 P.M. we sent Chris across the street to get answers.

As he walked across the street, Chris recognized a catering waitress on a smoke break in the garage. He pulled the girl, a friend of his sister's, aside and whispered, "When are the whores gonna get here?"

"What?"

"The whores? Mrs. Wagner said that there were going to be whores from Orvrays, Mexico, here."

The caterer looked puzzled for a minute, paused, and then grimaced. "You idiot. What Mrs. Wagner said was: h-o-r-s d-'o-e-u-v-r-e-s. Hors d'oeuvres, not whores de Orvrays, or whores from Orvrays."

"You mean they're not coming?" Chris said.

"Who?" said the caterer.

"The whores."

"No. You want a cheese straw?"

Chris wasn't listening. Despondent, he walked back over to the tree house and gave us the news.

The neighborhood slowly slipped back into its predictable routine. Ladies found new telephone-gossip topics, the Franklins fell into lockstep and switched to Scotch pine, and finger foods became finger foods again—although, for some strange reason, the term canapé fell into favor. My friends and I entered junior high at a new school and spent the next three years in search of female foreign-exchange students from Mexico. Mr. Johnson took a job in Dallas and, according to Mrs. Wagner, abandoned the banking trade to become a male model—that, or a frail bottle.

For years afterward, the men of the neighborhood could be seen cruising the streets at night in the family Chevrolet, always slowing at the Johnson house, a distant look of longing in their eyes.

Buffet Table

Fried Green Tomatoes with Shrimp Rémoulade

Virginia Ham and Pimento-Cheese Biscuits

Dirty-Rice Cakes Topped with Crawfish Mardi-Gras Mix

Cornmeal Biscuits with Fig Butter

Tasso-and-Cheese Biscuits with Pepper Jelly

Boiled Shrimp with Three Sauces

Crabmeat Imperial

Stone-Ground Catfish Curls with Tabasco-Tartar Sauce

Creole-Mustard-Crusted-and-Stuffed Pork Tenderloin

Broccoli Slaw

Snookie's Chicken Salad

Fried Green Tomatoes with Shrimp Rémoulade

The best of New Orleans paired with the Southern garden. The tomatoes should be fried at the last possible minute, since quality suffers as time moves on.

SHRIMP RÉMOULADE (*Yield: 2 cups*)
¼ cup celery, finely chopped
⅓ cup onion, finely chopped
½ cup ketchup
1½ Tbl lemon juice, freshly squeezed
1 Tbl prepared horseradish
½ cup homemade mayonnaise (page 193) or top quality store-bought
1½ Tbl Creole seasoning (page 205)
1 tsp Lawry's seasoned salt
½ tsp garlic, minced
2 tsp parsley, freshly chopped

1 cup cold boiled shrimp, roughly chopped

FRIED GREEN TOMATOES (*Yield: 2 cups*)
18 green tomato slices (approximately 3-4 large green tomatoes)
1½ cups seasoned flour, (page 208)
1½ cups egg wash (2 eggs beaten with 1 cups milk)
1½ cup bread crumbs
Cottonseed oil for frying (1-3 cups, depending on size of skillet or fryer used)

TIP for Entertaining

Keep dish-washing to a minimum. Use parchment paper as a liner for baking pans, casseroles, and pots. When finished, just wad up the paper and throw it away.

1. Place celery and onion into a mixing bowl. Add remaining ingredients, except shrimp, and blend well. Fold in the shrimp. Rémoulade sauce tastes better if made at least 1 day in advance.

2. Heat about 1 inch of oil to 350 degrees. Check temperature with a deep-fat thermometer.

3. Dip each tomato into flour, then into egg wash, then lightly coat with bread crumbs. Fry until golden brown. Drain on paper towels and hold in a warm oven at 175 degrees until all slices are fried.

4. Top with Shrimp Rémoulade and serve.

Virginia Ham and Pimento-Cheese Biscuits

Yield: 10-12 servings

I dare you to eat just twelve! It is rare that anyone ever has leftover pimento cheese, but if you do, these biscuits are a great way to finish it off. Use any one of the three pimento cheese recipes in this book.

2 cups self-rising flour
1 Tbl sugar
2 Tbl unsalted butter, cut into small
   pieces and chilled

¼ cup homemade pimento cheese,
   crumbled
⅔ cup buttermilk
2 Tbl butter, melted

1. Preheat oven to 375 degrees.
2. In a food processor, combine flour and sugar, and pulse to mix. Add butter and pimento-cheese pieces, pulsing until mixture resembles coarse bread crumbs. Transfer mixture to a large mixing bowl and make a well in the center. Pour buttermilk into the well and gently blend together the dough, being careful not to overmix.

TIP for Entertaining

Buy the best knife you can afford, keep it sharpened, and always use a cutting board. A dull knife is dangerous. To sharpen a knife properly, use a stone or steel rod, and run the blade along it at a forty-five-degree angle six times on each side.

3. Allow the dough to set for 10 minutes and then turn dough onto a floured surface. Gently knead dough for 1–2 minutes. Roll out to ¾-inch thickness.

4. Cut 1½-inch circles from the dough and place them on an ungreased baking sheet. Brush the tops with the melted butter.

5. Bake 12–15 minutes.

6. Cut biscuits in half lengthwise and lay a small piece of Virginia ham in the center. Serve warm.

Dirty-Rice Cakes Topped with Crawfish Mardi-Gras Mix

Yield: 20 cakes

The rice cakes can be made two days in advance, the topping one day in advance. After you have browned the dirty-rice cakes, you can hold them in the refrigerator for up to two days.

3 cups dirty rice, cooled (page 210)
¼ cup green onion, chopped
2 Tbl parsley, chopped
2 eggs, beaten
¼ cup coarse bread crumbs
1 cup Italian-bread crumbs
¼ cup unsalted butter

CRAWFISH MARDI-GRAS MIX
(Yield: Enough for 20 Dirty-Rice Cakes)
1 Tbl olive oil

½ cup red onion, minced
¼ cup red bell pepper, diced
¼ cup green bell pepper, diced
1 tsp garlic, minced
1 tsp salt
1 tsp Creole seasoning (page 205)
¼ lb cleaned crawfish tails, finely chopped
2 Tbl sour cream
1 Tbl Parmesan cheese

1. Preheat oven to 350 degrees.
2. In a food processor, pulse 1½ cups of the dirty rice. (Do not make a paste; the rice should just begin to resemble coarse bread crumbs.)
3. Place pureéd rice in a mixing bowl with the remaining rice, green onion, parsley, eggs, and plain bread crumbs. Mix well.
4. Form into 1½-inch round patties, approximately ¾-inch thick. Gently bread the cakes using the Italian-bread crumbs.
5. In a large sauté pan, melt butter over medium heat and brown cakes on both sides. Place browned cakes on a baking sheet.
6. Bake the cakes for 8–10 minutes.
7. Top warm rice cakes with crawfish mixture (below) and heat for 5 more minutes.
8. Place on serving dish and top with a small dollop of Roasted Red-Pepper Aioli (page 192).
9. For crawfish: Heat olive oil in a medium-sized skillet over medium-high heat. Add onion, red and green pepper, garlic, salt, and Creole seasoning, and cook 4–5 minutes. Let cool. Combine cooled vegetables, crawfish, sour cream, and Parmesan cheese.

To stop a green vegetable from cooking, and to help it retain its color, remove it from the boiling water and shock it in a bowl of ice water.

TIP for Entertaining

Cornmeal Biscuits with Fig Butter

Yield: 25-30 biscuits

Fig butter is addictive. It is the perfect accompaniment to spread on biscuits, batter breads, toast, croissants, or a loved one.

1½ cups all-purpose flour	¼ cup sugar
½ cup cornmeal	¼ cup solid vegetable shortening, cold
1½ tsp baking powder	¼ cup butter, chilled and cut into small
1 tsp salt	pieces
1 tsp poultry seasoning (page 207)	1 cup milk

1. In a large bowl, combine the flour, cornmeal, baking powder, salt, poultry seasoning, and sugar. Add the cold shortening and butter pieces and blend well, using your hands, until the mixture resembles coarse crumbs. Stir in the milk. The dough will be moist and sticky.
2. Dust a work surface with flour and cornmeal. Turn dough onto the floured surface. Gently fold each side toward the center. Flour surface again, and repeat process once more.
3. Using your hands, press the dough out until it is 1-inch thick.
4. Cut 1½-inch biscuits and place them on a lightly greased baking sheet. Let biscuits rest for 15 minutes before baking.
5. Bake in a 400-degree oven for 15 minutes, or until golden brown. Serve with Fig Butter (page 201).

Tasso-and-Cheese Biscuits with Pepper Jelly

Yield: 30-36 small biscuits

Experiment with the intensity of your pepper-jelly (page 182), the hotter the better. The dough freezes well and can be made in advance.

2 cups flour
1 Tbl sugar
½ tsp baking soda
2 tsp baking powder
1 tsp kosher salt
1 tsp black pepper, freshly ground
½ cup unsalted butter, chilled and cut into
   small pieces

¼ cup Cheddar cheese, shredded
¼ cup tasso ham, finely minced
¾ cup buttermilk
1 egg
2 Tbl butter, melted

1. Preheat oven to 375 degrees.
2. Combine all the dry ingredients in a large mixing bowl. Using a pastry-cutter or fork, blend the cold butter into the dry mixture until it resembles coarse bread crumbs. Mix in the cheese and the ham.
3. Separately, blend together the buttermilk and the egg and add to dry mixture. Blend the dough. Do not overmix.
4. Fold dough onto a floured surface and roll to a 1-inch thickness. Cut biscuits using a ½-inch cookie cutter. Place biscuits on ungreased baking sheet and brush the tops with the melted butter. Bake 15–18 minutes.

Boiled Shrimp with Three Sauces

Yield: Serves 10-12

After the smoked tenderloin, this is the second thing to disappear at a party. If you don't peel the shrimp in advance, they won't go as fast. Peel them and watch them fly.

3 qts water
5 Tbl salt
1 Tbl liquid crab boil
2 bay leaves
½ cup white wine
1 lemon, halved
5 lbs large shrimp, head and shell on

1. Place everything except the shrimp into an 8-quart stockpot. Bring the mixture to a simmer and cook for 5 minutes. Add the shrimp and cook for 5–7 minutes. Drain and spread the shrimp onto baking sheet pans, refrigerating immediately.
2. Serve with Comeback Sauce (page 196), Seafood Rémoulade Sauce (page 191), and Cocktail Sauce (page 198).

Keep a variety of pasta in the pantry. For an unexpected group of guests, sauté fresh vegetables, heavy cream, and Parmesan cheese to make pasta primavera.

TIP for Entertaining

Crabmeat Imperial

If you love crabmeat, you'll love this dish. If you don't love crabmeat, this dish will win you over. It's perfect when paired with champagne. Serve with toasted French-Bread Croutons (page 202) or buttery crackers.

1 Tbl butter
¼ cup yellow onion, small dice
¼ cup minced shallot
½ cup red pepper, small dice
¼ cup green pepper, small dice
¼ cup celery, small dice
¼ tsp salt
⅛ tsp cayenne pepper
1 Tbl garlic, minced
2 Tbl parsley, chopped
½ cup green onions, chopped

1½ cups homemade mayonnaise (page 193) or quality store-bought
3 Tbls Creole mustard
1 Tbl sherry vinegar
¼ tsp hot sauce
2 lb lump crabmeat
¼ cup dried panko bread crumbs
3 Tbl sour cream
2 tsp lemon juice
2 tsp Creole seasoning (page 205)
2 tsp chives chopped for garnish

TIP for Entertaining

Peeling celery removes its bitterness.

1. In a large sauté pan, heat the butter. When the pan is hot, add the onion, shallots, red and green pepper, celery, salt, and cayenne pepper. Sauté for 5 minutes or until the vegetables are soft and translucent. Add the garlic, parsley, and green onion, and sauté for 1 or 2 minutes. Remove from the heat and cool 30 minutes.
2. Preheat the oven to 400 degrees.
3. In a mixing bowl, combine 1 cup of the mayonnaise, mustard, vinegar, and hot sauce. Mix until thoroughly incorporated. Gently fold in the crabmeat. Spoon the mixture into an 8 x 8-inch baking dish.
4. In a separate bowl, combine the bread crumbs, the remaining ½ cup of mayonnaise, sour cream, lemon juice, and Creole seasoning together. Spread the bread crumb mixture on top of the crab mixture.
5. Bake 20 minutes, or until bubbly and brown. Garnish with chopped chives.

Stone-Ground Catfish Curls with Tabasco-Tartar Sauce

Yield: 6-8 servings

Catfish always tastes better when the portion size of the fish filets is thinner. Filleting the catfish horizontally and then slicing them lengthwise, creating "curls," accomplishes this task better than anything I've found. If possible, find locally milled stone-ground meal and keep it in the freezer. This preparation works when feeding a crowd at a fish fry, too.

Peanut oil for frying

1 lb catfish "curls"

1½ cups stone-ground cornmeal

½ cup corn flour

3 Tbl Lawry's seasoned salt

3 Tbl lemon pepper seasoning

Tabasco-Tartar Sauce (page 195)

TIP for Entertaining

To slice meat into paper-thin strips, partially freeze it and it will slice more easily. This works for catfish, too.

80

1. Using a deep-fat thermometer, heat 1 inch of oil in a cast-iron skillet to 350 degrees.

2. To make catfish "curls," take 5–7 oz catfish filets and place them in the freezer until they become half frozen. This makes them easier to slice. Cut the filets in half horizontally (your knife blade should run parallel to the cutting board). This creates a thin filet. Then cut the filet in half lengthwise, with the knife blade running perpendicular to the cutting board.

3. Combine the cornmeal, corn flour, Lawry's, and lemon pepper. Dredge catfish strips in the cornmeal mixture, making sure filets are evenly coated.

4. Carefully drop the strips into the fryer in small batches. Fry until golden (about 6 minutes), remove, drain, and serve.

5. Repeat the frying process until all the strips are fried. Serve immediately with Tabasco-Tartar Sauce.

Creole-Mustard-Crusted-and-Stuffed Pork Tenderloin

Yield: 6-8 servings

This dish is great on the buffet table and even better as an entrée at a dinner party.

2 Tbl raw bacon, finely chopped
¼ cup yellow onion, minced
½ cup mushrooms, finely chopped
½ cup Granny Smith apples, small dice
¼ tsp salt
¼ tsp black pepper, freshly ground
¼ cup Calvados

2 Tbl honey
2 Tbl Creole mustard
1 Tbl fresh thyme, chopped
¼ cup coarse bread crumbs
1 pork tenderloin, approximately 16-20 oz
¼ cup Creole mustard
Salt and pepper, to taste

1. Preheat oven to 400 degrees.
2. Place bacon in a medium-sized sauté pan over medium heat until brown. Add onion, mushrooms, apples, salt, and pepper. Continue to cook for 7–10 minutes. Deglaze with Calvados and cook until the liquid has evaporated. Remove from heat and add the honey, mustard, thyme, and bread crumbs. Cool mixture completely.
3. Lightly oil a large piece of foil, large enough to wrap the pork loin completely.
4. Using a sharp knife, butterfly the pork loin by making a ½-inch cut down the entire length of the loin. Fold the wider part away from the incision and repeat the same cut two more times. At this point, the pork tenderloin should lay flat.
5. Spread the apple mixture over the flattened pork loin. Roll it tightly and place on the oiled foil. Rub outside of the pork with Creole mustard and season lightly with salt and pepper, then wrap the entire roll in the foil.
6. Place wrapped pork on a baking sheet and bake at 400 degrees for 10 minutes. Lower the heat to 275, and cook an additional 10 minutes.
7. Remove from the oven and allow the pork to rest for 8–10 minutes. Gently remove the foil, then slice thinly on a diagonal and arrange on a platter.

still
need 1
line cut
space
is too
tight to
folio art

Broccoli Slaw

Your guests will need a fork, but they'll also need a bigger plate. The tiny broccoli florettes should be no larger than a thimble.

2 cups broccoli florettes, cut very small
2 cups broccoli stems, thinly julienned
½ cup green cabbage, finely shredded
½ cup red cabbage, finely shredded
½ cup carrot, shredded
¼ cup red onion, finely shaved

DRESSING
½ cup sugar
½ cup red wine vinegar

2 tsp Creole mustard
1 tsp horseradish
½ cup homemade mayonnaise (page 193) or top quality store-bought
2 Tbl sour cream
2 tsp lemon juice
1 tsp salt
¼ tsp black pepper, freshly ground

1. Bring one quart of lightly salted water to a boil.
2. Cook broccoli for 45 seconds, drain immediately, and run under very cold water. Use a paper towel to dry excess moisture from the broccoli.
3. Combine all the vegetables in a mixing bowl and add the dressing.
4. In a small stainless-steel saucepan, combine the sugar and the vinegar. Simmer slowly until the mixture forms a thick syrup.
5. While the mixture is cooking, combine the remaining ingredients in a mixing bowl and blend well.
6. Slowly drizzle the vinegar mixture into the mayonnaise mixture.

Snookie's Chicken Salad

Next to my grandmother's chicken salad, Snookie Foote's recipe is the best. Snookie was my surrogate grandmother, so I guess that's fitting.

2 lbs chicken breasts

2 tsp poultry seasoning (page 207)

1 onion, quartered

2 celery stalks

1 cup celery, chopped

1 bay leaf

1½ quarts water

4 eggs, hard-boiled and chopped

2 tsp Creole seasoning (page 205)

1 tsp Lawry's seasoned salt

¾ cup homemade mayonnaise (page 193) or top quality store-bought

2 Tbl Creole mustard

1 can water chestnuts, roughly chopped

½ cup pecans, toasted

½ cup celery, minced

¼ cup red onion, minced

1 Tbl lemon juice, freshly squeezed

¼ tsp black pepper, freshly ground

2–3 Tbl chicken stock

1. Place the chicken, poultry seasoning, onion, celery, bay leaf, and water in a large stockpot and bring to a boil. Lower heat and simmer until the chicken is cooked through. Remove chicken from pot, reserve broth, and cool.

2. Dice the cooked chicken and place in a large bowl to cool.

3. Add the remaining ingredients and mix well.

TIP for Entertaining

Chicken stock is the best base for soups, and homemade is best. When boiling a chicken for chicken salad, reduce the liquid by one third and freeze it in small portions.

The Wrath of Grapes

Larry Foote's Super Summer Sours

Souped-Up Gin and Tonic

Purple Parrot Mojito

Peach Daiquiri

Pimm's Royale

Purple Parrot Chocolate Martini

Jimmy McKenzie's Bloody Mary

Mary Virginia's Brandy Milk Punch

Swamp Water

Lava Lamps

Red Rooster

Planter's Punch

Beeson Punch

Presbyterian Punch

Episcopalian Punch

Catholic Punch

Baptist Punch

Mrs. Lampkin's Methodist Punch

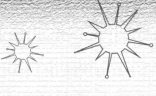

Larry Foote's Super Summer Sours

Yield: 4 drinks

1 eight-oz can frozen lemonade concen-
    trate
6 oz apricot brandy
2 oz Canadian Club whiskey

5 maraschino cherries
1 Tbl cherry juice
Ice

1. Place the lemonade concentrate, brandy, whiskey, cherries, and cherry juice in a blender. Fill with ice. Blend. Serve immediately, garnished with an orange slice and a cherry.

Souped-Up Gin and Tonic

Yield: 1 drink

1½ oz gin
4 oz tonic

1 tsp Mandarin Napoleon brandy
Squeeze of lime

1. Serve over ice.

TIP for Entertaining

Limit bar choices. For example, try serving champagne and beer only, or pitchers of infused spirits made with fresh berries or citrus fruits marinated in vodka or tequila.

Purple Parrot Mojito

12 leaves mint, fresh

2 oz light rum

1 oz lime juice, freshly squeezed

¼ oz simple syrup (½ cup sugar and ½ cup water, heated until dissolved)

Soda water to top

1. Using a muddler or the back of a spoon, muddle mint in the bottom of a cocktail glass. Add rum, lime juice, and simple syrup. Fill glass half full with crushed ice and stir well. Fill glass to the rim with more crushed ice and top with soda. Stir and serve, garnished with a sprig of mint.

Peach Daiquiri (Frozen)

Yield: 1 daiquiri

2 oz light rum

1 oz peach schnapps

1 oz lime juice, freshly squeezed

1 Tbl fresh peach, minced

½ oz simple syrup (as above)

1. In a blender, add all ingredients with plenty of ice. Blend well and serve in a hurricane glass garnished with a slice of fresh peach.

To chill a six-pack of beer or a bottle of wine quickly, fill a bucket with ice and add enough water to form a slush. When bottles or cans are submerged, the water should go halfway up the containers.

TIP for Entertaining

89

Pimm's Royale

1½ oz Pimm's No. 1 Cup
Champagne

1. In a champagne flute, pour one shot of Pimm's. Fill flute with chilled champagne and garnish with a julienned cucumber stick or fresh raspberries.

Purple Parrot Chocolate Martini

Yield: 1 martini

½ oz Absolut vodka
½ oz Kahlúa
¼ oz Godiva Dark Chocolate Liqueur

¼ oz Godiva White Chocolate Liqueur
1 Tbl half-and-half

1. In a cocktail shaker, add ice. Add liquor and liqueurs in order. Shake with ice and fine strain into a chilled martini glass.

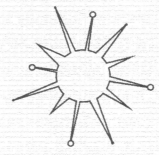

TIP for Entertaining

Champagne is best if it is chilled overnight.

Jimmy McKenzie's Bloody Mary

1 can V-8 (46 oz)
1 fifth vodka
4½ oz lemon juice (freshly squeezed)
¼ cup Worcestershire sauce

10 drops Tabasco sauce
2 tsp salt
1 Tbl black pepper, freshly ground
1 tsp sugar

1. Stir all ingredients well. Serve over ice garnished with a celery stalk, pickled okra, or spiced green bean.

Mary Virginia's Milk Punch

Yield: 4 drinks

½ cup brandy
⅔ cup bourbon
1 Tbl vanilla
100 gratings nutmeg

2 cups half-and-half
1 cup simple syrup (½ cup sugar and ½
        cup water, heated until dissolved)

1. Combine all in a quart container. Shake well. Keep refrigerated. Serve over ice.

The host or hostess is always served last.

TIP for
Entertaining

Swamp Water

1 part lemon juice
2 parts orange juice
Powdered sugar, to taste

1 part bourbon
1 part rum
Maraschino cherry (optional)

1. Mix, chill, and serve in cocktail glasses, garnished with cherry or orange slice.

Lava Lamps

Yield: 6-8 drinks

1 three-oz package instant Jell-O mix
   (red or blue)
1 cup boiling water

1 cup vodka
1 (750 milliliter) bottle champagne,
   chilled

1. In a medium bowl, stir together the gelatin mix and boiling water until completely dissolved, about 2 minutes. Stir in the vodka. Pour the liquid into small paper cups or portion cups. Chill until set, at least 2 hours.

2. Pour the champagne into glasses. Break up the gelatin with a fork and pour into a glass of champagne.

TIP for Entertaining

Plan for one glass per person, per hour; this will keep you from having to wash glasses during a party.

Red Rooster

1½ oz light rum

½ oz crème de noyaux

6 oz guava juice

Splash grenadine

1. In a Collins glass, add ice, add ingredients in order. Drink. Repeat, often.

Planter's Punch

Yield: 1 serving

1 oz rum

1 oz lime juice, freshly squeezed

½ oz grenadine

1 oz orange juice

1 tsp sugar

7UP

1. Fill a 12-oz Collins glass with ice. Add rum, lime juice, grenadine, orange juice, and sugar. Fill to top with 7UP.

The smart cocktail-party host offers an equal number of hot and cold food appetizers. While an hors d'oeuvre is heating in the oven, a cold appetizer should be making the rounds.

TIP for Entertaining

Beeson Punch

1 forty-six-oz can pineapple juice
1 small can frozen orange juice

1 small can frozen lemonade
1 qt ginger ale

1. Mix together all ingredients. Add enough water to make 1 gallon.
2. Serve in a punch bowl.

Presbyterian Punch

Yield: 70 four-oz
servings

This punch can be made in advance and frozen. Ice is not needed, as the partially thawed punch base will keep the ginger ale cool.

8 six-oz cans lemonade
3 qts water
1 forty-six-oz can unsweetened pineapple
   juice

3 qts ginger ale

1. Mix juices and freeze in 3 half-gallon milk cartons.
2. Thaw 3–4 hours, and add ginger ale.
3. Add 1 chilled bottle ginger ale to each ½ gallon of base.

TIP for Entertaining

Remember to chill wine, water, and other drinks on ice well in advance of the party.
Have a unique, non alcoholic specialty drink available for the designated driver of a group.

Episcopalian Punch

1 fifth bourbon, 100 proof
1 fifth brandy
1 fifth sherry
1 fifth sparkling red wine

Juice of 12 fresh lemons
2 cups sugar
1 fifth soda water

1. Combine all the ingredients except the soda water. Chill. Add soda just before serving.

Catholic Punch

½ gallon burgundy wine
1 pint gin
2 qts ginger ale

½ cup granulated sugar
¼ cup lemon juice

1. Mix 2 cups of the wine with the sugar to dissolve. Combine with rest of the wine and all the other ingredients in a large punch bowl and chill.

TIP for Entertaining

Before serving iced tea or minted punch, place a sprig of mint and a tiny lemon slice in each section of an ice cube tray, or ice ring, before freezing.

Baptist Punch

2 cups cranberry juice cocktail
2 cups apple cider
1 cup pineapple juice

1 cup orange juice
¼ cup lemon juice, freshly squeezed
2 qts ginger ale

1. Combine the first five ingredients and mix well. Chill. Just before serving, add the ginger ale.

Mrs. Lampkin's Methodist Punch

Yield: 32 4-oz portions

1 forty-eight-oz can pineapple juice
1 three-oz package instant lime gelatin
  mix

1½ cups sugar
1 cup lemon juice, freshly squeezed
1 small bottle almond extract

1. Mix all the ingredients in a gallon-sized container and fill with water to make one gallon. Chill.

When preparing punch, make half the recipe and freeze in a ring mold. Float the ring in punch when serving. For an added treat, add fruit to the mold before freezing.

TIP for Entertaining

Around and About the House

Mild Mississippi Cheese Straws

This is the best cheese-straw recipe ever created. When served fresh out of the oven, they can't be beat. Add a little extra cayenne to make them even better than the best.

½ lb sharp Cheddar cheese, shredded
½ lb white Cheddar, shredded
2 cups all-purpose flour, sifted
½ cup butter, softened
1 tsp salt
⅛ tsp cayenne pepper
⅛ tsp black pepper, freshly ground

1. Preheat oven to 375 degrees.
2. Process all ingredients in a food processor for 30 seconds or until the mixture forms a ball.
3. On a floured surface, roll out the dough to a ¼-inch thickness. Cut into 4-inch straws, ½-inch wide, and place on an ungreased baking sheet.
4. Bake for 8–10 minutes. Best when served directly out of the oven.

TIP for Entertaining

Keep cheese in the refrigerator, tightly wrapped in plastic, away from air flow. Air grows mold on cheese. If mold forms on the outside, just trim it off.

Fiery Cheese Straws

These aren't as fiery as the name states. Add some more cayenne and watch your guests storm the bar.

1 lb sharp Cheddar cheese, shredded
2 cups all-purpose flour, sifted
½ cup butter, softened
½ tsp salt
¼ tsp cayenne pepper
½ tsp Creole seasoning (page 205)
⅛ tsp black pepper, freshly ground
1 tsp hot sauce

1. Preheat oven to 375 degrees.
2. Process all ingredients in a food processor for about 30 seconds; the mixture should form into a ball.
3. On a floured surface, roll out the dough to ¼-inch thickness. Cut into 4–5-inch straws, ½-inch wide, and place on an ungreased baking sheet.
4. Bake for 8–10 minutes. Best when served right out of the oven.

Sesame Cheese Straws

Sesame is a long-time staple of the Southern larder and a perfect partner with cheese straws.

1 lb sharp Cheddar cheese, shredded
2 cups all-purpose flour, sifted
½ cup butter, softened
1 tsp salt
½ tsp cayenne pepper
1 tsp sesame oil
½ cup sesame seeds, toasted

1. Preheat oven to 375 degrees.
2. Process all ingredients in a food processor for about 30 seconds or until the mixture forms a ball.
3. On a floured surface, roll out the dough to a ¼-inch thickness.
4. Cut into 4–5-inch straws, 1-inch wide, and place on an ungreased baking sheet. Bake for 8–10 minutes.

Deep-South Party Mix

This is my twist on party mix. The chapter title is deceptive, as these can't really be left out around the house for too long because they'll disappear before the party even starts. But put a few bowls of these out and you'll make a lot of folks happy. Fry in small batches so the oil temperature doesn't drop too severely, which would result in a greasy finished product.

Peanut oil for frying

2 cups yellow cornmeal

3 Tbl Lawry's seasoned salt

3 Tbl lemon pepper seasoning

½ cup jalapeños, sliced

½ cup dill pickle slices

½ cup okra, sliced

½ lb crawfish tails, cleaned

1¼ cups egg wash (2 eggs beaten with 1 cup milk)

1. Using a deep fat thermometer, heat about 1 inch of oil in cast-iron skillet to 350 degrees.
2. Combine cornmeal, Lawry's, and lemon pepper.
3. Dredge the jalapeños, pickles, okra, and crawfish in the egg wash, then in the cornmeal mixture. Carefully drop the dredged items into the fryer in small batches. Fry until golden (about 6 minutes), then remove and drain.
4. Repeat until everything has been fried.
5. Serve immediately.

Store spices in a cool, dark place. Humidity, light, and heat cause herbs and spices to lose their flavor. Never keep spices above the stove.

TIP for Entertaining

Cajun-Spiced Nuts

Yield: 1 quart

These are great when made in large batches and given as Christmas gifts.

2 Tbl bacon grease or canola oil
2 tsp fresh garlic, finely chopped
1½ cups dry-roasted, unsalted peanuts
1 cup pecan halves
1 cup walnut pieces
1 cup whole, unsalted cashews

1 cup whole, unsalted almonds
1 Tbl Creole seasoning (page 205)
2 tsp salt
1 Tbl sugar
2 tsp black pepper, freshly ground

1. Preheat oven to 175 degrees.
2. In a small sauté pan, melt the bacon grease over low heat. Add the garlic and cook for 3–4 minutes. Do not brown the garlic. Place all nuts in a large mixing bowl. Drizzle the bacon grease and garlic mixture over nuts and toss well to coat evenly.
3. Sprinkle seasonings and sugar over the nuts in small batches, tossing nuts to distribute seasonings evenly.
4. Pour nuts out onto a large baking sheet and place in the oven. Cook for 45 minutes, stirring every 10 minutes.
5. Remove nuts from oven and allow to cool completely.
6. Store in an airtight container before serving.
7. Spiced nuts will hold for 4–5 days.

As a general rule, herbs and ground spices will retain their flavor for one year. Whole spices can last three to five years. Proper storage will result in a longer shelf life.

TIP for Entertaining

Sugared Peanuts

Yield: 6 cups

As a kid, I never ate the peanuts in my box of Cracker Jack, opting for the caramel-coated popcorn only. If the peanuts had tasted like these, I wouldn't have had any reservations.

2 Tbl butter
2 cups sugar
¼ tsp salt
1 lb roasted, unsalted peanuts

1. In a large sauté pan, melt butter over medium-low heat. Stir in ½ cup of the sugar and the salt, and cook until it begins to turn a light tan (it will also begin to melt slightly). Stir in peanuts, mixing well in hot sugar mixture. Sprinkle another ½ cup of the sugar, mixing constantly. Cook 4–5 minutes. Repeat process until all sugar has been added to the peanuts, constantly stirring the nuts to prevent uneven cooking or burning.
2. When cooled completely, store in an airtight container.
3. Can be served warm or at room temperature.

TIP for Entertaining

Don't store herbs and spices in the refrigerator, as it is humid. However, spices can be stored in the freezer in a tightly sealed container.

Holiday Popcorn

You'll have to fight the kids for this one. Better still, make a double batch and share. It can be made ahead and stored in an airtight container for two weeks.

8 cups popcorn, popped
¾ cup pecans, chopped and lightly
   toasted
1 cup slivered almonds, lightly toasted

1 cup butter
1½ cups sugar
½ cup corn syrup
2 tsp vanilla extract

1. Place the popcorn and the toasted nuts in a very large mixing bowl and hold in a warm area while preparing the caramel coating.
2. Melt the butter in a heavy-duty saucepan and stir in the sugar and the corn syrup. Cook slowly, stirring often, until mixture reaches a rich brown color. Remove from the heat and whisk in the vanilla extract. Be careful—the caramel is hot and sticks to the skin if spilled.
3. Drizzle one-half of the caramel over the popcorn mixture and gently toss, mixing well. Add the remaining caramel and mix again.
4. Pour popcorn onto a wax-lined cookie sheet and cool completely. Gently break up the popcorn before serving.

For slow-cooking dishes, add the herbs and spices an hour or less before serving. Cooking spices too long may result in overly strong flavors.

TIP for Entertaining

Cheddar-Rice Cookies

These can be prepared to the just-before-baking stage and then frozen. They're perfect when served at an afternoon tea.

2 cups flour
¼ tsp Creole seasoning (page 205)
½ tsp dehydrated onion
⅛ tsp black pepper, freshly ground
¼ tsp salt

1 cup unsalted butter, softened
½ lb extra-sharp Cheddar cheese
¼ tsp hot sauce
2 cups Rice Krispies

1. Preheat the oven to 325 degrees.
2. Combine the flour and the dry seasonings in a mixing bowl and blend well.
3. Place the butter, cheese, hot sauce, and Rice Krispies in the bowl of an electric mixer. Using the paddle attachment, blend mixture, slowly adding the flour and seasonings, until all flour is incorporated and moistened.
4. Form into small balls (approximately ¼–½ oz) and place on a baking sheet. Bake 15–20 minutes.

TIP for Entertaining

White plates are the best backdrop for food and garnishes.

The Payback Party of 1976

My mother loves all things Early American and would, if given the chance, travel back to the eighteenth century to live in Colonial Williamsburg.

A devout member of the Daughters of the American Revolution and the Colonial Dames, Williamsburg is her Mecca, the center of her universe. It guides her travel, it influences her reading. It is the basis for every decorating decision she has ever made or will ever make. No matter what the problem is, the way they did it in Colonial times is the solution.

My mother loves Williamsburg almost as much as she hates dirty hands. She is not phobic, but she watches too much television, committing every news report involving germs or dirt to memory, and within hours publishes lengthy theses on cleanliness, which she passes out to every member of the family.

Her love of all things Early American is in her bloodstream, and molds her philosophy. She wanted her two sons to grow up and attend the College of William and Mary, not because of any concern for our education, but for its proximity to Colonial Williamsburg.

So on that fateful day in 1976 when she announced that she was planning a party, my brother and I already knew the theme.

Three years earlier, she had dragged us along on one of her many pilgrimages to the Early American Promised Land. We went willingly, but only based on the promise that we would also be able to go to Busch Gardens and ride the roller coaster.

We arrived in Colonial Williamsburg at the crack of dawn. Nothing had opened yet, but she didn't want to risk missing a single thrill that might lie waiting in the simulated replica of an Early American village. As we walked through the streets, I witnessed a transformation in her demeanor. She was wide-eyed and in awe. Weaving our way through the James Geddy House, she spoke under her breath, to no one in particular, "Things were just better back then."

"But Mom, they peed in a bowl and kept it on a table in their room overnight."

"It's called a chamber pot, and just look at the craftsmanship and artistry of the bowl. It's beautiful. Anyone would be proud to urinate in such a work of art. I'll bet they always kept their hands clean."

"But Mom, they had no air-conditioning."

"It was cooler back then, boys. Those were the days before global warming." My mother, unlike the colonists, was early into environmental issues.

She bought us tricornered hats and made us wear them. It was 1973—the year in which bell-bottoms reached their largest circumference and stack shoes attained their highest elevation—but there we were, at twelve and sixteen years old, wearing tricornered hats and souvenir-shop baby-blue waistcoats with our names stitched on the chest.

After the obligatory photograph of my brother and me locked in the stocks, and a visit to the town pillory, we went to the blacksmith shop, where she bought me a horse-shoe. "Did you wash your hands? You don't know where that horseshoe has been."

"But I do know where it's been, Mom. It's been with us in the un-air-conditioned blacksmith shop for the last two and a half hours."

After visiting a basket-maker, a shoemaker, a brick-maker, and a wig-maker, we ended up watching a woman churn butter. No Busch Gardens. "You boys can ride a roller coaster anytime. This is history. Now, go wash your hands."

Three years later, this trip would pay off as we prepared for the Williamsburg party. The Colonial theme would be easy to create, as the house would need no decorating. We lived in my mother's own private Williamsburg.

The house was painted Colonial yellow, and all the rooms were adorned with antiques and reproductions from the Early American era. While our friends had posters of Dennis Hopper, Peter Fonda, and the Beatles hanging in their rooms, our rooms were filled with framed prints of Minutemen, Ben Franklin, and Thomas Jefferson. The bathroom my brother and I shared was a patriotic tribute to the Founding Fathers—a blue lavatory, a white shower, and a red commode. Yes, a red commode.

I can trace 42 percent of the difficulties in life to having to use a fire-engine-red commode for the first eighteen years of my life. Immediately after she built the house, I tried to explain to her that the citizens of Colonial Williamsburg never had to sit on red toilets.

"They were extremely patriotic," she replied. "If they had ever had the chance to sit on a red commode, I'll just bet they would have."

On the day of the party, my mom found the hiding place where we had hidden the tricornered hats. She made us wear them during the event. My brother opted for his brown leisure suit, figuring it would at least make him look like a modern-day American statesman.

The party was a "payback party." A payback party is a social gathering one holds to pay back all of the people who have invited one to a party over the course of the previous year. She was three years overdue in her payback, as she had been waiting for the perfect time to host her next party—the Bicentennial.

The rooms were themed: The living room became the Boston Tea Party, where her silver tea service was placed on a mahogany secretary. Constitution Hall was the entry hall where my brother manned the coat closet. The Raleigh Tavern and Public House was the breakfast room where the bar was set up, and the dining room was the Governor's Palace.

My brother made an eight-track mixed tape—his version of Colonial-themed music—for the occasion. The party mix included such hits of the day as "Play That Funky Music" by Wild Cherry, "Afternoon Delight" by the Starland Vocal Band, "Car Wash" by Rose Royce, "Don't Go Breakin' My Heart" by Elton John and Kiki Dee, "Muskrat Love" by the Captain and Tennille, and "Free Bird" by Lynyrd Skynyrd. I loaned him my forty-five single of Edwin Starr's "War" to add to the lineup in the hope that it might conjure up images of the American Revolution. The mood was now set.

I was churning butter in the Governor's Palace as the guests began to arrive. The house filled quickly, due to the three-year delay in party payback.

While the rooms were crowded, it was mostly quiet on the food front. Colonial food, having its roots in the cuisine of Mother England, didn't lend itself to memorable dining. The cloth-draped table was full of such Early American delectables as salt mackerel, pickled cabbage, rice pudding, preserved fruit compote, corn pone, fermented-lemon chess pie, something called George Washington Cherry Surprise, Monticello gingerbread, and six different recipes using cranberries as the main ingredient.

"Mom, I don't think that George Washington Cherry Surprise is a true Colonial dish."

"Well, they would've eaten it had they known about it. Did you wash your hands before churning that butter?"

The typical bone china, crystal, and sterling silver had given way to the more true-to-theme pewter and copper.

As KC and the Sunshine Band played over the hi-fi system, cocktails were being served in large pewter mugs that weighed at least three pounds each. The sheer weight of the drinks forced serious pleasure-seekers to stay close to the bar, which allowed them to get seriously drunk. Those brave enough to venture through the house with a weighty mug full of faux ale and a bulky pewter plate full of salt mackerel and cranberries were so tired by the time they reached the family room that they called it quits and went home to eat a more fitting, and less exhausting, supper.

Many of the guests weren't into the Colonial theme. Most skipped the ale and headed straight for the scotch—another import from the British Isles—and never complained.

Over the years, my mother had purchased and inherited an impressive collection of Early American antique furniture. Unfortunately, most of the pieces were old and delicate, and off-limits for sitting, not to mention uncomfortable. As the evening wore on, and the scotch and ale began to produce their desired effects, my mother nervously scurried around the house trying to keep drunken—and now rowdy—guests from dancing on the small handmade chairs and tables.

From my spot at the butter churn, I could see my brother dancing the robot in his tricornered hat as "Play That Funky Music" blared over the tinny speakers in the Market Square/family room.

"You'll never get into William and Mary acting like that," my mother yelled to him as she pulled a pressed-tin lampshade off of a neighbor's head in the corner of the Raleigh Tavern.

With the food being a major disappointment, the highlights of the party appeared to be the endless supply of scotch from the liquor cabinet, and the red commode in the front bathroom, which hosted a steady stream of gawkers for most of the evening. "Come see, Sarah, they have a red commode!"

Overall, the payback party served its purpose. The corner grocery finally got rid of their three-year-old salt mackerel inventory, our friends' parents learned how to dance the robot, my brother and I gained a newfound respect for our red toilet, and we were finally able to mothball the tricornered hats in the back closet, where they've remained for thirty years.

My mother recently moved into a condominium, "a townhouse just like the Guardhouse in Williamsburg," she says. It is filled with all of the Early American antiques that survived the Payback Party of 1976.

Out of the Freezer

Shrimp Empanadas

Chicken-and-Andouille Empanadas

Miniature Crawfish Pies

Baked Shrimp Toast

Sausage-and-Cheddar Ryes

Supper Bread

Baked Cheese Treats

Baked Cheese Puffs

Shrimp Empanadas

These are the perfect frozen party food. Keep a batch in the freezer and, when unexpected company shows up, pop them in the oven. They'll wonder how you made something that tastes so good, and looks so complicated, so quickly.

¼ lb fresh shrimp	¼ tsp salt
1 tsp blackening seasoning	½ tsp ground cumin
1 tsp Old Bay seasoning	½ tsp chili powder
½ tsp salt	1 tsp Creole seasoning (page 205)
1 Tbl olive oil	1 tsp black pepper, freshly ground
1 Tbl bacon fat	¼ cup cream cheese, softened
⅓ cup red onion, minced	2 tsp hot sauce
1 Tbl garlic, minced	2 Tbl green onion, thinly sliced
¼ cup red bell pepper, minced	2 Tbl cilantro, finely chopped
1 Tbl jalapeños, minced	1 recipe Easy Pastry (page 208)

1. Toss the shrimp in the blackening seasoning, Old Bay, and ½ tsp salt.

2. In a medium-sized sauté pan, heat the olive oil over high heat and sauté the seasoned shrimp until pink and cooked through. Remove shrimp from the pan and cool completely. Finely chop the chilled shrimp and place in a mixing bowl.

3. In a separate sauté pan, heat the bacon fat over medium heat. Sauté the onion, garlic, peppers, and salt for 1–2 minutes. Stir in the cumin, chili powder, Creole seasoning, and black pepper and cook 1 more minute. Remove from heat and cool completely.

4. In the bowl with the shrimp, add the onion mixture, cream cheese, hot sauce, green onions, and cilantro. Once cooled, add the vegetable mixture, blend well, and refrigerate until firm.

5. Roll the Easy Pastry out until paper thin. Cut pastry using a 3-inch cookie cutter. Place 1–1½ tsp of the shrimp filling in the center of each circle. Gently fold the circles in half and pinch the edges together to seal the pastries.

6. Place the pastries in the freezer on a baking sheet until they are completely frozen. Once frozen, place in airtight bags or containers to store.

7. If preparing without freezing, chill the pastries 30 minutes in the refrigerator before baking.

8. To cook: Preheat the oven to 350 degrees. Place pastries on a paper-lined baking sheet and brush with egg wash (1 egg mixed with 2 Tbl of water). Bake for 18–20 minutes.

When serving peeled or shelled seafood, have extra bowls on the table for discarded shells, and have lemon-scented finger bowls and warm towels available so guests can keep their hands clean.

TIP for Entertaining

Chicken-and-Andouille Empanadas

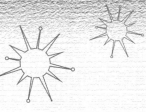

There are a lot of ingredients in this recipe, but don't let that discourage you from making these easy pastries. Measure out all the ingredients ahead of time and your job will be much easier. These are perfect for those times when you have misjudged bulk-food quantities when hosting a party; keep a batch in the freezer and, when the food starts running low, pop them in the oven.

2 Tbl bacon fat

½ cup andouille sausage, finely diced

¼ cup onion, minced

½ tsp salt

¼ cup green chilies, minced

1 Tbl garlic, minced

½ tsp ground cumin

1 tsp chili powder

¼ tsp cayenne pepper

¼ tsp dried oregano

¼ tsp ground coriander

2 Tbl tequila

½ cup chicken, cooked and finely diced

2 tsp hot sauce

¼ cup sharp Cheddar cheese, finely grated

¼ cup Pepper Jack cheese, finely grated

1 recipe Easy Pastry, (page 208)

1. In a medium sauté pan, heat bacon fat over medium-high heat. Add sausage and brown 4–5 minutes. Add onion and salt, and cook 3–4 minutes more, stirring often.

2. Add in the chilies, garlic, and seasonings and cook 2 more minutes. Deglaze with the tequila. Add the diced chicken and allow the tequila to cook out of mixture. Remove from heat and cool in a mixing bowl.

3. Once the mixture is cool, fold in hot sauce and cheeses. Before forming the empanadas, refrigerate mixture 1–2 hours or until firm.

4. Roll the Easy Pastry out until paper thin. Cut pastry using a 3-inch round cookie cutter. Place 1–1½ tsp of the chicken filling in the center of each circle. Gently fold the circles in half and pinch edges together, sealing the pastries. Chill the pastries for 30 minutes before baking.

5. Place pastries on a baking sheet in freezer until completely frozen. Once frozen, place in airtight bags or containers to store.

6. To cook: Preheat oven to 350 degrees. Place pastries on paper-lined baking sheet and brush with egg wash (1 egg with 2 Tbl water). Bake 18–20 minutes.

To remove stains from nonstick cookware, boil two table-spoons of baking soda, one-half cup of vinegar, and one cup of water for ten minutes. Season the pan with salad oil before the next use.

TIP for Entertaining

Miniature Crawfish Pies

As a party rule, passed hors d'oeuvres move more slowly than foods arranged on trays and placed on a table. This recipe might disprove that theory. They don't have to be frozen to be enjoyed; cook before freezing for an instant treat. If you don't have any of the Pepper-Jelly Dipping Sauce made, substitute pepper jelly.

1 tsp bacon fat
⅓ cup onion, minced
1 tsp garlic, minced
3 Tbl celery, finely chopped
¼ tsp cayenne pepper
¼ tsp black pepper, freshly ground
1 tsp salt
¾ cup cream cheese, softened

2 Tbl Pepper-Jelly Dipping Sauce (page 182)
2 Tbl cilantro, chopped
2 Tbl green onions, finely sliced
2 tsp soy sauce
½ lb crawfish tails, drained well and finely chopped
1 recipe Easy Pastry (page 208)

1. In a medium-sized skillet, melt the bacon fat over medium heat. Cook the onion for 3–4 minutes. Do not brown. Add the garlic and celery and cook approximately 1 minute. Remove from the heat and stir in the cayenne, black pepper, and salt. Transfer to bowl of an electric mixer and allow to cool. Add the Pepper-Jelly Dipping Sauce, cilantro, green onion, and soy sauce to mixing bowl. Using the paddle attachment, combine ingredients on low speed. Remove from mixer and fold in the crawfish. Cover and refrigerate.

2. Roll out pastry dough to a ⅛-inch thickness. Use a 3-inch cookie cutter to cut out circles.

3. Place approximately 1½ tsp of the filling in the center of the dough circles and fold in half. Pinch the edges, sealing pies.

4. Place pies on a baking sheet in freezer until completely frozen. Once frozen, place in airtight bags or containers to store.

5. To cook: Preheat oven to 375 degrees. Place pies on a baking sheet and cook 10–12 minutes.

Rub hands with parsley to remove chopped garlic or onion odors.

TIP for Entertaining

Baked Shrimp Toast

Always use freshly grated Parmesan cheese. Never use that powdery stuff that comes in a can. Use Pepper-Jelly Dipping Sauce (page 182), Plum Sauce (page 190), or Muscadine Sauce (page 184) with this recipe.

1 qt water

1 tsp crab boil

1 tsp salt

1½ cups small shrimp, (approximately 10 oz)

1 eight-oz package cream cheese

1 Tbl onion, finely minced

½ cup homemade mayonnaise (page 193) or top quality store-bought

¼ cup sour cream

½ tsp garlic, minced

¼ cup Parmesan cheese, freshly grated

1 tsp Creole mustard

2 Tbl green onions, finely chopped

1 tsp hot sauce

¼ tsp Old Bay seasoning

⅛ tsp cayenne pepper

1 small loaf French bread, cut into 1½-inch rounds

1. In a saucepan, bring the water, crab boil, and salt to a boil. Cook the shrimp thoroughly, drain, and cool. When shrimp has cooled, rough chop into small pieces.
2. Combine all the remaining ingredients except the French bread. Add shrimp.
3. Spread a thick layer of the shrimp mixture onto the French bread rounds. Place rounds on a baking sheet and freeze. When completely frozen, transfer to an airtight plastic bag.
4. To cook: Preheat oven to 350 degrees. Remove from freezer. Place on baking sheet and cook 15 minutes.

Sausage-and-Cheddar Ryes

These are perfect with cocktails when unexpected guests show up.

1 lb ground beef

1 lb hot breakfast sausage

¼ cup onion, finely minced

¼ cup red bell pepper, finely minced

1 Tbl garlic, minced

½ lb sharp Cheddar cheese, shredded

½ lb cream cheese

¼ cup green onion, finely minced

2 tsp Creole seasoning (page 205)

1 tsp Worcestershire sauce

1 tsp Tabasco sauce

1 loaf miniature rye bread

1. Brown ground beef and sausage, cooking thoroughly. Drain excess fat and add onion, pepper, and garlic. Cook 4–5 more minutes. Remove from heat and allow mixture to cool.
2. While mixture is cooling, combine remaining ingredients in the bowl of an electric mixer. Using the paddle attachment, blend until well incorporated. Add beef-sausage mixture and slowly blend once more.
3. Spread mixture evenly (about ¼-inch thick) onto slices of the miniature rye.
4. Freeze on sheet pans and then transfer to airtight plastic bags.
5. To cook: Bake at 350 degrees for 10–12 minutes.

Supper Bread

Grocery-store freezers are filled with premade cheese-and-garlic-laden bread loaves. Do yourself a favor and make your own. This recipe is a perfect place to start.

½ cup butter

¼ cup yellow onion, minced

2 tsp garlic, minced

1 Tbl Creole mustard

1 tsp yellow mustard

1 tsp black pepper, freshly ground

2 tsp Creole seasoning (page 205)

¼ cup bacon, cooked, finely chopped

2 Tbl fresh parsley, finely chopped

¾ cup mozzarella cheese, grated

¾ cup Swiss cheese, grated

1 large loaf French bread (long but narrow)

1. Melt the butter in a small sauté pan over low heat. Cook the onion and the garlic 5 minutes. Do not brown. Remove from the heat and stir in the mustards, Creole seasoning, and black pepper. Set aside.

2. In a large mixing bowl, combine the cheeses, bacon, and parsley.

3. Cut French bread into 1-inch-thick slices, on a diagonal. Do not cut all the way through the bottom of the loaf. (The loaf may need to be cut in half to fit in a freezer.)

4. Place the French bread on a large sheet of foil and distribute the cheese mixture between the diagonal slices. Drizzle butter mixture over the loaf, making sure that it goes into the center of the slices. Rub the mixture over the entire surface of the bread.

5. Wrap the loaf in the foil and freeze.

6. To cook: Preheat oven to 350 degrees. Remove bread from oven and allow to sit for 15–20 minutes. Bake 20–25 minutes.

Baked Cheese Treats

1 large loaf French bread

½ lb sharp Cheddar cheese, grated

½ lb white Cheddar cheese, grated

¾ cup homemade mayonnaise (page 193) or top quality store-bought

¼ cup sour cream

3 Tbl whipping cream

1 tsp Creole seasoning (page 205)

2 Tbl green onion, minced

1 tsp lemon juice, freshly squeezed

1 Tbl red onion, minced

1 tsp Worcestershire sauce

½ tsp black pepper, freshly ground

¼ cup Parmesan cheese, shredded

1. Preheat oven to 400 degrees.

2. Remove crust from the French bread. Cut bread into 1½-inch-thick circles, then cut the circles in half, creating half-moon-shaped slices.

3. In a mixing bowl, combine the remaining ingredients (except the Parmesan cheese) and mix well. Top the pieces of bread evenly with the cheese mixture and place on a baking sheet lined with parchment paper.

4. Refrigerate for 30 minutes, or until ready to serve, or freeze until ready to use.

5. Sprinkle the bread with the shredded Parmesan and bake 5 minutes.

6. Can be held warm for 20–30 minutes.

Baked Cheese Puffs

Yield: 40 puffs

½ lb Old English cheese
½ cup solid vegetable shortening
½ cup butter, softened
2½ cups self-rising flour
1 Tbl hot sauce

1 tsp Creole seasoning (page 205)
1 cup toasted almonds, chopped
1 Tbl parsley, chopped
1 Tbl paprika

1. Using an electric mixer, blend together the Old English cheese, shortening, and butter until well blended. Add the remaining ingredients except paprika and mix well until all ingredients are incorporated.
2. Refrigerate dough for 1 hour.
3. Using a small (1½–2 ounce) ice-cream scoop, form small balls and place onto a baking sheet. Freeze raw dough balls in ziplock bags until ready to use.
4. Remove cheese balls from freezer. Sprinkle with paprika and bake 20–30 minutes, until golden brown.

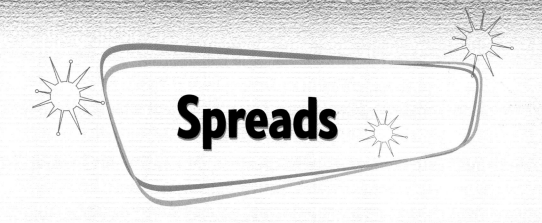

Spreads

Pimento Cheese . . . The Pâté of the South

There as many versions of pimento cheese as there are cooks who cook with pimento cheese. In my circle of family and friends, there are many different ideas of how pimento cheese should be prepared—hence, the three different recipes in this book.

12 oz sharp Cheddar cheese, shredded and at room temperature
¾ cup Parmesan cheese, grated
½ cup roasted red pepper, diced
½ cup homemade mayonnaise (page 193) or top quality store-bought

1 tsp Creole seasoning (page 205)
1 tsp hot sauce
1 tsp Worcestershire sauce
1 tsp garlic powder
2 tsp dehydrated onion

1. Using the paddle attachment of an electric mixer, combine all ingredients until well blended.
2. Cover and refrigerate for at least 2–3 hours, allowing flavors to combine.

Pimento Cheese 2

This pimento cheese recipe was inspired by the groundbreaking Southern chef Bill Neal.

12 oz aged white Cheddar cheese, shredded and at room temperature
¾ cup Parmesan cheese, freshly grated
½ cup roasted red peppers, medium dice
⅓ cup homemade mayonnaise (page 193)
2 tsp horseradish
1 tsp Creole seasoning (page 205)

½ tsp hot sauce
¼ tsp chili powder
⅛ tsp ground cumin
⅛ tsp black pepper, freshly ground
1 tsp bourbon
1 tsp Worcestershire sauce
1 tsp garlic powder
2 tsp dehydrated onion

1. Using the paddle attachment of an electric mixer, combine all the ingredients until well blended.
2. Cover and refrigerate for at least 2–3 hours, to allow flavors to combine.

Pimento Cheese 3

This recipe includes bacon—not a typical pimento-cheese ingredient—which adds a nice smokiness.

½ cup cooked bacon, chopped

½ pound extra-sharp white Cheddar, roughly grated and at room temperature

½ pound extra-sharp yellow Cheddar, roughly grated and at room temperature

1 cup roasted red bell pepper, chopped

¾ cup homemade mayonnaise (page 193) or top quality store-bought

½ cup green onions, chopped

2 tsp garlic, minced

2 tsp Creole seasoning (page 205)

Salt

Black pepper, freshly ground

1. In a large skillet, cook the bacon until brown and crisp, 6–7 minutes. Transfer to paper towels to drain and cool. Using the paddle attachment on an electric mixer, combine the bacon with all the remaining ingredients until well blended.
2. Cover and refrigerate for at least 2–3 hours to allow flavors to meld.

TIP for Entertaining

Always keep a sense of humor.

Kentucky Beer Cheese

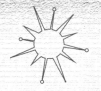

My brother, who lives in Kentucky, introduced me to beer cheese. It is a staple of the bars and pubs of the Bluegrass state.

1 lb sharp Cheddar cheese, finely shredded
1 lb Swiss cheese, finely shredded
1 tsp dry mustard
¼ tsp black pepper, freshly ground

¼ tsp hot sauce
½ tsp garlic, minced
1 tsp Worcestershire sauce
1 cup dark beer

1. Place all ingredients into the bowl of an electric mixer and mix well, using a paddle attachment.
2. Divide mixture into six 8-oz containers and wrap well in plastic wrap. Age the beer cheese for 4–5 days before serving.
3. Before serving, allow the cheese to come to room temperature.
4. Serve with crackers or toasted rye-bread points.

Boursin

This is the recipe we serve in the Crescent City Grill. In addition to being a good spread for crackers, it can also be used to stuff mushroom caps, and as a filling for miniature puff-pastry turnovers.

8 oz cream cheese, softened
1 Tbl salted butter, softened
½ tsp Creole seasoning (page 205)
¼ tsp garlic, minced
⅛ tsp thyme, oregano, rosemary, chives, basil, dill, or sage

1 tsp fresh parsley, finely chopped
2 Tbl half-and-half
1 tsp sherry vinegar
¼ tsp Worcestershire sauce
⅓ cup sour cream

1. Place all the ingredients in the bowl of an electric mixer. Using the paddle attachment, beat on high speed, scraping sides of the bowl occasionally, until all ingredients are combined.

Smashing with the flat side of a knife works best, but you can microwave garlic cloves for ten seconds to get the skin to slip right off.

TIP for Entertaining

Barbara Jane's Layered Cream-Cheese Spread

This takes some work, but it is worth the effort. Mango chutney can be substituted for the peach preserves.

2 Tbl olive oil

¼ cup onion, minced

1 tsp garlic, minced

1½ tsp Creole seasoning (page 205)

1 ten-ounce package frozen spinach, thawed and squeezed dry

1 lb sharp Cheddar cheese, grated

⅓ cup homemade mayonnaise (page 193) or top quality store-bought

3 Tbl sour cream

½ cup toasted pecans, chopped

1 Tbl Creole mustard

1 Tbl parsley, chopped

2 eight-ounce packages cream cheese, softened

¼ tsp salt

½ tsp black pepper, freshly ground

⅛ tsp cayenne pepper

½ cup peach or apricot preserves

¼ cup green onion, minced

¼ tsp ground nutmeg

TIP for Entertaining

A block of cream cheese is a Southern cocktail-party staple. Top the block with: pepper jelly, chutney or caviar.

1. Line a 9 x 5-inch loaf pan with plastic wrap.
2. Heat the olive oil in a medium-sized sauté pan over medium heat. Cook the onions for 3–4 minutes. Stir in the garlic and the Creole seasoning, cooking 2 more minutes. Stir in the spinach and blend well. Remove mixture from heat and allow to cool.
3. In a mixing bowl, stir together the Cheddar cheese, mayonnaise, sour cream, toasted pecans, Creole mustard, and parsley. Blend very well, and spread half of this mixture into the bottom of the lined loaf pan.
4. In a separate bowl, combine one package of the cream cheese and the cooled spinach mixture. Blend well and spread over the halved Cheddar-pecan layer of the loaf.
5. Next, spread the remaining Cheddar mixture into the loaf pan.
6. Using the paddle attachment of an electric mixer, beat the remaining cream cheese until light and creamy. Add salt, black pepper, cayenne pepper, preserves, green onion, and nutmeg. Spread the final layer into the loaf pan and wrap very tightly with plastic wrap.
7. Refrigerate for 4–6 hours before serving. (Also freezes well; must thaw 8 hours before serving.)
8. To serve, sink the loaf pan into a warm-water bath for 1–2 minutes. Do not let water seep into plastic and reach mold. Unmold onto serving platter and remove plastic wrap.

Garlic-Cheddar Spread

Garlic is listed first for a reason. Store in the refrigerator and serve at room temperature.

1½ tsp garlic, finely minced

½ lb sharp Cheddar cheese, grated

½ lb cream cheese, softened

¼ tsp salt

1½ tsp hot sauce

1 tsp Worcestershire sauce

2 tsp homemade Mayonnaise (page 193)
 or top quality store-bought

¼ tsp dry mustard

1½ tsp paprika

1. In a food processor or mixing bowl with a paddle attachment, blend all of the ingredients together.
2. Cover and refrigerate for 3–4 hours before serving.

TIP for Entertaining

To make garlic oil: Add two cloves of garlic, peeled and sliced, to one cup of olive oil. Store in a sealed, glass jar in the refrigerator.

It Ain't a Party Until Someone Breaks Out a Block of Cream Cheese
Yield: enough for 10-12 guests

My friend Julia Reed says, "You would never see a naked block of cream cheese in the South. It will always be coated with one of at least three delicious things: Pickapeppa sauce, Jezebel sauce, or pepper jelly." In honor of Julia, these recipes take the dumping-a-jar-of-pepper-jelly-on-top-of-a-block-of-cream-cheese staple to another level.

1 eight-ounce block cream cheese

PEACH TOPPING
¾ cup peach preserves
⅛ tsp cayenne pepper
½ tsp crushed red-pepper chili flakes
¼ tsp paprika
Pinch of salt

ORANGE TOPPING
¾ cup orange marmalade
1 Tbl horseradish
2 tsp Worcestershire sauce
¼ tsp white pepper
1 Tbl sour cream

BLUEBERRY TOPPING
¾ cup blueberry preserves
1 Tbl shallot, finely minced
2 tsp balsamic vinegar
2 tsp cornstarch
1 tsp black pepper, freshly ground
⅛ tsp cayenne pepper

1. For peach and orange topping, combine all the ingredients. Top cream cheese with half of the mixture. Reserve other half to pour over cream cheese as the topping is consumed.

BLUEBERRY TOPPING

1. Heat preserves and shallots over medium heat until the mixture begins to simmer. Combine the vinegar with the cornstarch and stir it into simmering preserves. Remove from the heat and stir in the peppers. Cool completely. Top cream cheese with half of the mixture. Reserve other half to pour over cream cheese as the topping is consumed.

Methodists and the Art of Cat-Flossing

n the South, parties come in all shapes, forms, sizes, and scopes. They are held in apartments and homes, on lawns, patios, porches, and verandas.

Whether city or country, beachside or poolside, Southerners are just as comfortable at a barbecue, crawfish boil, or pig-picking as they are at a seated brunch, cocktail party, formal gala, or black-tie ball.

Parties are also held in churches—not just holiday teas in the parsonage, and post-nuptial wedding receptions in the church parlor, but the ultimate, end-all, and coup de grace of Southern cooking: the covered-dish supper.

I am a Methodist, and we Methodists love a covered-dish supper.

A covered-dish supper is a mass-feeding event in which a select group of people bring a portable dish for many to share. Enough dishes are brought so that a collection of families have plenty of food from which to choose. In the South, it is an opportunity for the home cook to shine. Though in a church, the covered-dish supper has a definite party atmosphere surrounding it.

At my church, every mother in every family brought a dish. Some ladies excelled in desserts, some in vegetables, others in the main course. No one ever brought chain-store chicken or grocery-store cakes. The food was always made from scratch, and was always good. The atmosphere at these gatherings was light, festive, and full of hope and eager expectation.

Tables ran the entire length of the fellowship hall for the once-a-week feast, and every red-checkered inch was filled with a homemade specialty. My church

never hosted a we'll-supply-the-meat, you-bring-the-vegetables-and-dessert covered-dish supper. The ladies in my church brought the center-of-the-plate items, too: fried chicken, meatloaf, main-course casseroles, side-dish casseroles, and dessert casseroles.

Casseroles have become the redheaded stepchild of the Southern larder. In these days of micro greens, boutique vinegars, and designer foams, casseroles have taken a backseat to the trendy foods-of-the-moment. It is a sin, indeed.

An honest casserole is true comfort food. As long as we can wean ourselves off of canned-soup fillers and other shortcut additions, the Southern casserole is as legitimate as any French cassoulet.

The casserole sits in an honored place of reverence at a covered-dish supper. The tables are a jungle of casseroles. From elaborately prepared entrées to cream-soup-laden vegetables, the dishes come in all sizes, shapes, and colors. Aromas rise from beneath the tin foil, fuse, and drift through the room, teasing the arrival of the imminent feast. It is at that moment—just before the foil is lifted and the single-file line begins to move forward—that the entire room smells Southern.

There is always a slight health risk involved in covered-dish suppers, due to the fact that most of the items are being held at room temperature for long periods of time. But Methodists—even though we're not known for living on the edge—would never let something as trivial as a bacteria-laden-food-borne illness get in the way of a successful covered-dish supper.

The covered-dish supper is also about fellowship. Sitting down with one's family, friends, and neighbors and enjoying a shared meal is a treat that has unfortunately become less common over the years. We pull through the drive-through window and bring home a paper sack full of fast-food fried chicken, and eat it on a TV tray while watching TV reality programs, and call it "dinner." Not so, the covered-dish supper.

As a child, some of my fondest food memories are centered in the fellowship hall of the Main Street United Methodist Church in my hometown of Hattiesburg, Mississippi. In my church, I knew who the best cooks were, and I always kept a close eye on the door when those women made their entrance. I knew who cooked the best fried chicken and who baked the finest homemade cakes. I arrived at church early on covered-dish-supper night and sat at a strategic location that offered a full and unobstructed view of the food tables. From my perch, I watched closely to note the exact placement of the best-tasting dishes, making mental notes so I could return to load my plate with those items.

There is a certain conversational roar that overtakes a room when a crowd

is gathered and waiting to eat. The banter level gains a tinge of excitement. On covered-dish-supper night, the room was always alive and in full conversational roar. From my seat, I listened to the volume of the room as it raised and lowered, depending on which woman entered and which dish she was carrying. The entrance of a gifted cook bearing a banana-cream pie with homemade meringue piled eight inches above the custard made the room's noise level swell in anticipation. A woman lugging a strawberry shortcake made with store-brought whipped topping and leftover cornbread brought the noise level down a few decibels as an audible disappointment spread across the room.

In my church, there was an elderly woman who had a houseful of cats. I will call her Mrs. Lancaster, may she rest in peace. Mrs. Lancaster's cats were known to climb all over her kitchen counters and in and out of her cabinets. They ran wild in the streets and lived in, on, under, and on top of her house. It was not unusual to find a few dozen cat hairs in any casserole Mrs. Lancaster brought to a covered-dish supper.

When the Widow Lancaster walked into the fellowship hall on covered-dish-supper night, the conversational roar came to a halt and the crowded room fell instantly silent. All eyes focused on her. The entire membership watched in measured stillness as she slowly shuffled across the room and placed her casserole on the table among the other offerings. The room's silence was quickly replaced by frantic whispers. "Pass the word; it's a congealed green-bean ring tonight." Once the location of the dish was noted, the room once again filled with chatter, and the parade of casseroles entering the room resumed.

I pitied the latecomers who weren't in the room when Mrs. Lancaster arrived, for they were clueless when it came to trying to figure out which dish was hers. Later, I watched with great delight as the uninformed and out-of-the-casserole-loop church members ate, occasionally pulling strands of a thin, string-like substance from between their teeth. I called this covered-dish-supper practice "cat-flossing."

Up North, covered-dish suppers are called potluck dinners. The food is bland and tasteless. Northerners sit around eating unseasoned meat and talk about how much snow they shoveled that morning. Down here, in the epicenter of the Bible

Belt, we have parties in churches where we eat fried chicken, potato salad, green bean casserole, broccoli casserole, chicken and dumplings, chicken pie, barbecue ribs, butter beans, peas, cornbread, yeast rolls, assorted pies, homemade ice cream, and coconut cakes, while simultaneously keeping a close eye on church members who own more than three cats.

Cold Dips

Curried-Crab Dip with Vegetable Fritters

Smoked-Crab Dip

Cilantro-Spiked Corn, Crab, and Avocado Dip

Eggplant and Roasted-Garlic Dip

Spicy-Shrimp Dip

MegaGuacamole

Southern Hummus

Smoked-Salmon Spread

Summer Garden Dip

Three-Mushroom Dip

Hot-Pepper Cheese Dip

Curried-Crab Dip with Vegetable Fritters

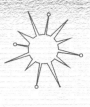

Yield: 25-30 fritters

This is the yin-and-yang recipe of this book: Hot-cold, sweet-savory, vegetable-fish—all of which lead to one of my favorite recipes.

CURRIED CRAB DIP (*Yield: 1 quart*)

1 Tbl vegetable oil

1 Tbl garlic, minced

1 Tbl Madras curry powder

¼ cup sour cream

½ cup buttermilk

1 cup homemade mayonnaise (page 193) or top quality store-bought

2 Tbl mango chutney

1 green onion (white and green), thinly sliced

2 tsp hot sauce

1 tsp lime juice, freshly squeezed

2 Tbl red bell pepper, small dice

1 Tbl rice vinegar

1 tsp salt

½ tsp cayenne pepper

1 Tbl fresh cilantro, finely chopped

½ lb crabmeat (claw meat works well in this recipe)

VEGETABLE FRITTERS

1 cup flour

1 tsp salt

1 tsp Creole seasoning (page 205)

1 Tbl baking powder

1 egg

½ cup buttermilk

⅓ cup milk

2 Tbl bacon fat, melted

½ cup zucchini, coarsely shredded

¼ cup carrot, shredded

¼ cup broccoli florettes, finely chopped

1 Tbl green onion, minced

1 tsp garlic, minced

Oil for frying

Salt to taste

1. Heat the oil in a small skillet over medium heat. Add the garlic and cook about 2 minutes. Do not brown. Add the curry and cook, stirring, until fragrant, about 30 seconds more. Set aside and cool.

2. In a bowl, combine the sour cream, buttermilk, curry mixture, mayonnaise, chutney, green onion, vinegar hot sauce, lime juice, salt, pepper, and cilantro, and mix well. Gently fold in the crabmeat, and chill before serving.

3. Serve with vegetables fritters (below). (Crackers or chips work well, too.)

4. In a large bowl, combine the flour, salt, Creole seasoning, and baking powder. In a separate bowl, mix together the egg, buttermilk, and milk. Fold the wet ingredients into the dry and mix until just blended. Do not overmix. Gently fold in the melted bacon fat and vegetables. Add the garlic.

5. Heat about 1 inch of oil to 375 degrees. Check temperature with a deep-fat thermometer.

6. Gently drop 1–1½ Tbl-sized spoonfuls into the hot oil, frying only a few at a time. Cook until golden brown. Remove from the oil, and allow to drain on a plate lined with paper towels. Sprinkle with salt. Serve immediately.

Don't crowd food when frying. Fry in small batches. Food must be surrounded by oil, and the temperature of the oil can't drop too low or the food will be greasy and soggy.

TIP for Entertaining

Smoked-Crab Dip

Yield: 2 cups

One of the most intensely flavored and deeply satisfying dips you will ever try. Smoking the crab is easy, and is extremely important to the outcome of the dip. This is a great dip for a party. It also travels well. Pack a small container full of the crab dip in an ice chest, make a batch of Herbed Pita Triangles (page 212), and take them to the beach. Add the other half pound of crabmeat for a more intense smoke-and-crab flavor.

½ cup cream cheese, softened
½ cup sour cream
1½ tsp horseradish
2 Tbl red onion, minced
2 Tbl celery, minced
2 Tbl parsley, chopped
1 Tbl lemon juice, freshly squeezed
1 tsp garlic salt
1½ tsp Creole seasoning (page 205)

¼ tsp black pepper, freshly ground
1 Tbl hot sauce
½ lb smoked lump crabmeat (below)

SMOKED CRABMEAT

1 lb crabmeat, picked clean of all shell
1-2 cups wood chips, soaked for 1-2
   hours in water

1. Blend the softened cream cheese and the sour cream with the paddle attachment of an electric mixer until there are no lumps.
2. Add in all the other ingredients except for the smoked crab, and blend well. Gently fold in the smoked crab by hand. Chill for 3–4 hours before serving.

3. Prepare a very small amount of charcoal according to the manufacturer's directions. Place one pound of crabmeat in a colander and place the colander on a small metal baking sheet. Sprinkle one-quarter of the wood chips onto the glowing charcoal, and place the baking sheet with the colander on top onto the grill in your smoker or barbecue. Place the crabmeat as far from the heat as possible (crabmeat is already cooked). Be careful not to dry out the crabmeat during the smoking process. Smoke 40 minutes, adding new wood chips every 10 minutes. Remove the crab from the smoker and chill completely before making the dip.

Keep flower arrangements on the dinner table low to the table so guests can keep eye contact and easily hold conversations. On a buffet table, make arrangements as large as you like.

TIP for Entertaining

Cilantro-Spiked Corn, Crab, and Avocado Dip

Yield: 12-14 guests

Corn, crab, and avocado work well when grouped together in a cold offering. The cilantro adds an additional coolness, which makes this the perfect summer dip.

2 Tbl tequila

3 Tbl lime juice, freshly squeezed

¼ cup olive oil

1 tsp salt

1 Tbl hot sauce

⅛ tsp cayenne pepper

3 avocados

1½ cups corn, freshly cooked and cut from the cob (use frozen kernels if fresh is not available)

2 Tbl red bell pepper, finely diced

1 tsp garlic, minced

¼ cup onion, finely chopped

1 cup fresh lump crabmeat, picked clean of all shell

1 Tbl cilantro, freshly chopped

1. Combine tequila, lime juice, olive oil, salt, hot sauce, and cayenne pepper in a mixing bowl.

2. Peel and cut the avocados into a small dice, then quickly place it in the lime juice mixture, tossing well so avocado is well coated.

3. Fold in the remaining ingredients.

TIP for Entertaining

A dampened paper towel or dishcloth brushed downward on a cob of corn will easily remove the silk.

Eggplant and Roasted-Garlic Dip

Yield: 3 cups

This is my wife's favorite dip in this book. It's great with French-bread Croutons (page 202).

2 medium-sized eggplants
1 cup olive oil
½ cup roasted garlic purée
2 tsp Creole seasoning (page 205)
2 Tbl sherry vinegar

1 Tbl fresh basil leaves, chopped
2 tsp fresh thyme
2 tsp black pepper, freshly ground
1 cup seeded tomatoes, small dice
½ cup green onion, thinly sliced

1. Preheat oven to 350 degrees.
2. Peel the eggplants. Take one and a half of the eggplants and cut into a large dice. Toss with half of the olive oil and place eggplant on a baking sheet. Roast 12–15 minutes or until golden brown and tender.
3. While the eggplant is roasting, take the remaining eggplant and cut into small uniform dice. Heat 2 Tbl of olive oil in a large sauté pan over high heat and sauté until tender (not soggy). Set aside.
4. Place the remaining olive oil, large-dice roasted eggplant, Creole seasoning, vinegar, basil, thyme, and black pepper into a food processor and purée until smooth. Fold in the diced tomatoes, eggplant, and green onions.
5. Store in an airtight container in the refrigerator.

To seed tomatoes, cut them in half and use your fingers or the tip of a spoon to remove the seeds and watery flesh.

TIP for Entertaining

Spicy-Shrimp Dip

This can also be spread on miniature bread slices for canapés and finger sandwiches.

¾ lb fresh shrimp, medium-sized

2 tsp Old Bay seasoning

½ tsp blackening seasoning

1 Tbl olive oil

¼ cup white wine

½ lb cream cheese, softened

½ cup sour cream

½ cup celery, finely chopped

¼ cup red onion, minced

¼ cup green onion, minced

1 Tbl jalapeños, minced

1 Tbl hot sauce

1 Tbl lemon juice, freshly squeezed

¼ tsp cayenne pepper

1 Tbl parsley, chopped

1 tsp salt

1. Toss the shrimp in the Old Bay and blackening seasoning.
2. Heat oil in a sauté pan over medium heat. When pan is hot, sauté shrimp until pink and cooked through. Remove shrimp from the pan and cool. Deglaze pan with the white wine, using a rubber spatula to remove seasoning from the pan.
3. Place the cream cheese into a mixing bowl of an electric mixer. Add the wine and sour cream. Using the paddle attachment, beat until smooth.
4. Add the cooled shrimp and remaining ingredients to the cream cheese mixture and mix until everything is well incorporated.

Nothing tastes as good as freshly boiled shrimp. But if you are in a pinch and need to save time, purchase ready-cooked, peeled, and deveined shrimp.

TIP for Entertaining

MegaGuacamole

My four-year-old son could take a bath in this stuff. After eating a serving, he sometimes looks like he has.

1 tsp lemon juice, freshly squeezed

1 Tbl lime juice, freshly squeezed

½ tsp garlic, minced

1½ tsp kosher salt

1 tsp black pepper, freshly ground

1 tsp hot sauce

1 Tbl sour cream

4 ripe avocados

½ cup red onion, finely chopped

1 Tbl cilantro, finely chopped

½ cup tomato, seeds removed, small dice

1. Combine the lemon and lime juice, garlic, salt, pepper, hot sauce, and sour cream and blend together well.

2. Remove the skin and seeds from the avocados and rough chop the pulp. Quickly fold the avocado pulp into the citrus mixture. Fold in the remaining ingredients.

TIP for Entertaining

Mash avocados with salsa for instant guacamole. Add fresh cilantro and some freshly minced garlic to store-bought salsa for a homemade taste. One bunch of parsley or cilantro without the stems is about one cup, chopped.

Southern Hummus

You may never use chickpeas for hummus again. Pink-eyed purple-hull peas will work, too. Tahini is a paste made from ground sesame seeds and can be found in specialty markets. There is no substitute for the tahini—it makes the recipe.

2 tsp garlic, minced
1 tsp salt
2 cups black-eyed peas, cooked
1 cup tahini, well stirred
2 Tbl lemon juice, freshly squeezed

¼ cup olive oil
½ cup water, plus extra, if needed
¼ cup parsley leaves, freshly chopped
¼ cup pine nuts, lightly toasted

1. Using a blender, purée all the ingredients except for the parsley and pine nuts. Add the water only as needed to keep the purée from becoming too thick. Store in an airtight container in the refrigerator.
2. Before serving, garnish with chopped parsley and toasted pine nuts. Serve with Herbed-Pita Triangles (page 212).

Smoked-Salmon Spread

Yield: 8-10 servings

All of the usual accoutrements are here, although in a different form. This recipe must be made one day in advance. Smoked trout may be used instead of salmon.

8 oz smoked salmon, thinly sliced

8 oz cream cheese, softened

½ cup sour cream

½ cup homemade mayonnaise or top
    quality store-brought

1 tsp hot sauce

¼ tsp Old Bay seasoning

1 tsp Dijon mustard

2 Tbl lemon juice, freshly squeezed

⅛ tsp Creole seasoning (page 205)

½ cup green onions, minced

¼ cup capers, chopped

¼ cup parsley, chopped

2 Tbl dill, freshly chopped

½ tsp black pepper, freshly ground

1. Line a 4-cup round mold with plastic wrap. Using half of the salmon slices, make a star pattern on the plastic wrap. Chop the remaining salmon into ½-inch pieces and set aside.
2. In the bowl of an electric mixer, combine the cream cheese, sour cream, and mayonnaise until creamy and well combined. Add the hot sauce, Old Bay seasoning, mustard, lemon juice, and Creole seasoning, stirring well.

TIP for Entertaining

Use hollowed-out vegetables as containers for your dips. They add color and shape.

160

3. Into the bowl, fold in the chopped salmon, green onions, capers, parsley, dill, and pepper. Place cream cheese mixture into lined mold. Cover with plastic wrap and chill until firm, about 3 hours.

4. To serve, place the bottom of the mold in a bowl of warm water for 10 seconds. Remove all plastic wrap and invert mold onto a serving plate, gently shaking to release.

5. Serve with toasted French-Bread Croutons (page 202), Herbed Pita Triangles (page 212), or Lemon-Pepper Dipping Crackers (page 211).

Summer Garden Dip

This is not a dish for leftovers; use the freshest vegetables available. It must be served within two days.

1 cup cottage cheese
½ cup homemade mayonnaise (page 193) or top quality store-bought
½ cup sour cream
¼ cup buttermilk
1 tsp Dijon mustard
2 tsp hot sauce
1 tsp garlic, minced
1 tsp lemon juice
1 tsp lemon pepper seasoning
1 tsp poultry seasoning, (page 207)
½ tsp black pepper, freshly ground
2 tsp fresh dill, finely chopped

½ tsp salt
2 Tbl green onion, minced
2 Tbl red bell pepper, finely chopped
2 Tbl carrot, coarsely grated
¼ cup fresh tomato, seeds removed, medium dice
¼ cup zucchini, finely shredded
¼ cup fresh corn, freshly cooked and cut from the cob (use frozen if fresh is not available)
2 Tbl frozen spinach, thawed, excess moisture removed

1. Blend together the cottage cheese, mayonnaise, sour cream, buttermilk, mustard, hot sauce, garlic, lemon juice, lemon pepper, poultry seasoning, pepper, dill, and salt. Mix well.
2. Fold in the vegetables.
3. Refrigerate for 4 hours before serving.

Three-Mushroom Dip

2 Tbl olive oil

1 cup medium mushrooms, finely chopped

1 cup shiitake mushrooms, finely chopped

1 cup portobello mushrooms, finely chopped (make sure mushrooms have been well cleaned)

1 tsp salt

¼ cup yellow onion, finely minced

1 Tbsp garlic, minced

¼ cup brandy

2 Tbsp dry ranch dressing seasoning mix

1 tsp poultry seasoning (page 207)

1 tsp black pepper, freshly ground

1 Tbsp Dijon mustard

¼ cup sour cream

¾ cup homemade mayonnaise (page 193) or top quality store-bought

1 Tbsp red wine vinegar

¼ cup green onion, thinly sliced

1. In a large sauté pan, heat the oil over medium heat. Place the mushrooms, salt, onion, and garlic into the sauté pan and cook for 6–7 minutes, stirring often. Add in the brandy and cook for 3–4 more minutes; there should be about ¼ cup of liquid remaining in the pan.

2. Remove from heat and cool.

3. In a mixing bowl, combine seasonings, mustard, sour cream, mayonnaise, and vinegar and blend well.

4. Fold in the mushroom mixture and the green onion.

When buying mushrooms, make sure stems and caps are attached and firm.

TIP for Entertaining

Hot Pepper Cheese Dip

Old English cheese comes in a jar and is in the refrigerator section along-side all of the other cheese. It's fake cheese, but it works well in this application. This is a great use for leftover pimento cheese.

1 cup sharp Cheddar cheese, finely shredded

1 seven-oz jar Old English cheese

½ cup homemade pimento cheese (page 132, 133, or 134)

8 oz cream cheese, softened

2 Tbl canned jalapeños, finely minced

1 tsp garlic, minced

½ tsp black pepper, freshly ground

½ tsp Creole seasoning (page 205)

½ cup toasted pecans, finely chopped

1 Tbl fresh parsley, chopped

1. Place the four cheeses into a food processor and blend until smooth. Add the remaining ingredients and blend until well incorporated.
2. Wrap tightly in plastic and refrigerate overnight.

TIP for Entertaining

To toast pecans and almonds, spread in one layer on a baking sheet and bake at 300 degrees until slightly brown, approximately 10 minutes. Stir often.

Hot Dips

Black-Eyed Pea Dip

Oyster-and-Artichoke Dip

Crawfish Cardinale

Not Your Ordinary, Average, Everyday Cheese Tart

Seafood au Gratin

Corn-and-Crab Dip

Spinach-and-Pepper-Jack Dip

Four-(or Five-) Cheese Dip

Sin Bread

Black-Eyed Pea Dip

I don't have enough adjectives stored in my computer to describe how much I like this dip. It's Southern, it's cheesy, it's hot, and it's tasty. Who needs more? I like to eat this dip with store-bought wheat crackers.

1 Tbl bacon fat or canola oil
½ cup yellow onion, minced
1 Tbl garlic, minced
2 tsp Creole seasoning (page 205)
½ tsp salt
1 ten-oz can Rotel tomatoes with chilies

2 cups black-eyed peas, cooked
½ cup Pepper Jack cheese, grated
½ cup Velveeta cheese, cubed
½ cup roasted red bell pepper, small dice
¼ cup green onion, minced

1. In a small sauté pan, heat the bacon fat over medium-high heat. Cook onions for 3–4 minutes. Add in the garlic, salt, Creole seasoning, Rotel tomatoes, and black-eyed peas. Simmer for 5 minutes. Cool slightly. Purée the pea mixture in a blender.
2. Combine the puréed mixture with the cheeses and heat over a double-boiler, stirring often. When cheeses have melted, fold in the roasted bell pepper and green onion.
3. Serve warm.

TIP for Entertaining

Drain black-eyed peas and dried beans after soaking, then shock with cold water before completing the recipe.

Oyster-and-Artichoke Dip

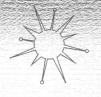

Yield: 1 quart

Oysters and artichokes are classic New Orleans pairings. One of the most popular soups served at our restaurants is Oyster and Artichoke Bisque. This recipe uses that soup as inspiration.

1 cup oysters, freshly shucked
¼ cup oyster liquor
½ cup milk
¾ lb cream cheese, softened
½ cup Parmesan, freshly grated
⅓ cup green onion, chopped
2 tsp garlic, minced
2 large eggs, beaten

1 Tbl lemon juice, freshly squeezed
1 cup drained, jarred, or thawed artichoke
   hearts, patted dry
1 tsp salt
2 tsp Creole seasoning (page 205)
¼ tsp black pepper, freshly ground
1 Tbl hot sauce
Butter, as needed

1. Preheat oven to 350 degrees.
2. Place the oysters in a small, stainless-steel sauce pot with the oyster liquor and milk. Simmer 6–7 minutes until oysters are thoroughly cooked. Strain, reserve liquid, and allow oysters to cool. Once cooled, roughly chop the oysters.
3. In a food processor, combine the cream cheese, reserved oyster broth, Parmesan, green onions, garlic, eggs, and lemon juice, and pulse until smooth. Add the artichokes, salt, Creole seasoning, pepper, and hot sauce, and pulse until just mixed. Fold in the chopped oysters by hand.
4. Transfer the mixture to a buttered, deep 1-quart casserole dish and bake until lightly browned and set, approximately 30 minutes.
5. Serve warm with crackers.

Crawfish Cardinale

A staple from my catering days. This can also be spread on slices of French bread, topped with shredded cheese, and baked.

3 Tbl unsalted butter	¼ cup sherry
¼ cup shallots, minced	1 Tbl lemon juice, freshly squeezed
½ cup onion, finely chopped	½ tsp salt
2 tsp garlic, minced	1 tsp Creole seasoning (page 205)
3 Tbl all-purpose flour	¼ tsp black pepper, freshly ground
2 Tbl tomato paste	1 lb boiled crawfish tails, roughly chopped
2 cups heavy cream	¼ cup green onion, chopped
¼ cup white wine	1 Tbl parsley, chopped

1. In a large sauté pan, melt the butter over medium-high heat. Add the shallots, onion, and garlic, and cook, stirring often, until soft, about 3 minutes. Add the flour and cook for 2 more minutes, stirring constantly. Add the tomato paste and cook 1 more minute. Add the wine and sherry and cook 3–4 minutes. Whisk in the cream, lemon juice, salt, pepper, and Creole seasoning and cook for 6–7 more minutes. Stir often to prevent sticking. Add the crawfish tails and cook until warmed through, 2–3 minutes.
2. Sprinkle with the green onion and parsley just before serving.
3. Serve with French-Bread Croutons (page 202) for dipping.

TIP for Entertaining

To crisp lettuce: Place the head in a bowl of ice-cold water with a slice of fresh lemon. Let it stand for an hour in the refrigerator and then pat dry with a paper towel.

Not Your Ordinary, Average, Everyday Cheese Tart

This is one of the easiest recipes in the book. There are a lot of versions of this recipe floating around; this is mine. It is not a true tart for many reasons, but that's what I call it. Once you taste it, you'll love it, and you can call it whatever you like.

2 Tbl unsalted butter
2 cups onion, diced
1 cup shallots, minced
1½ tsp salt
1 tsp black pepper, freshly ground
1 lb cream cheese, softened

½ lb white Cheddar, grated, room temperature
1 cup homemade mayonnaise (page 193) or top quality store-bought
2 tsp hot sauce
1 tsp garlic, minced

1. Preheat oven to 425 degrees.
2. Heat the butter in a large sauté pan over medium heat. Place the onion, shallots, salt, and pepper in the pan. Slowly cook the onion mixture, stirring often, until caramelized, with a rich brown color.
3. Place all the ingredients into a mixing bowl and stir until the mixture becomes smooth and creamy.
4. Spoon into a shallow soufflé dish. (Recipe can be made two days ahead of time and refrigerated at this point.)
5. Bake for 15 minutes.
6. Serve with croutons or crackers.

Seafood au Gratin

Here is a great use for fresh seafood scraps. Don't feel bound to use these exact seafoods; use what you have in the fridge. If you have more of one type than another . . . go for it. This can also be served as a lunch entrée, baked in an oven-proof ramekin and served with a light salad. There are a lot of ingredients, but the end result is worth the effort.

MORNAY SAUCE
6 Tbl butter, divided in half
2 Tbl all-purpose flour
¼ cup yellow onion, medium dice
1 cup milk, warm
1 cup heavy cream, warm
2 oz Swiss or Gruyère cheese, grated
¼ cup Parmesan cheese, grated
2 oz cream cheese
¾ tsp salt
¼ tsp cayenne pepper
1 tsp hot sauce
1 tsp lemon juice, freshly squeezed
¼ tsp nutmeg, grated

¼ pound fresh fish pieces, roughly
   chopped
¼ lb shrimp, peeled, deveined, and
   roughly chopped
2 tsp Old Bay seasoning
¼ cup white wine
¼ lb crawfish tails, roughly chopped
¼ lb crab claw meat
1 cup bread crumbs
2 Tbl mixed fresh herbs, finely chopped
2 Tbl Parmesan, grated
½ tsp black pepper, freshly ground
2 Tbl olive oil

1. Make a light-blond roux by melting half of the butter in a small saucepan over medium heat. Stir in the flour and increase heat to medium-high. Cook for 2 minutes. Do not brown. Add the onion and cook 3–4 minutes, stirring often to prevent roux from browning. Whisk in the milk and the heavy cream and cook, stirring constantly, until the mixture comes to a gentle boil. Cook until the floury taste is gone and sauce is smooth and thickened, about 3 minutes. Add

the Gruyère, Parmesan, and cream cheese and stir until melted. Season with salt, cayenne pepper, hot sauce, lemon juice, and nutmeg. Remove from heat.

2. Preheat oven to 350 degrees.

3. In a separate sauté pan, heat the remaining butter over medium heat. Season the fish and shrimp with Old Bay. Sauté the seafood until cooked through. Deglaze with the wine and allow liquid to evaporate. Stir in the crawfish and crabmeat and gently fold seafood into Mornay.

4. Pour into a 1½-quart baking dish.

5. In a small bowl, combine the bread crumbs, chopped herbs, Parmesan cheese, pepper, and olive oil. Sprinkle over the seafood mixture and bake for 20 minutes.

6. Allow to sit for 10 minutes before serving.

Grease pans with vegetable shortening.
It won't burn and stick like butter.

TIP for Entertaining

Corn-and-Crab Dip

The Corn-and-Crab Bisque served at our restaurants is a recipe that we have been serving from day one. As with the Oyster-and-Artichoke Dip, this dish gets its inspiration from my restaurants' top soup offering.

½ cup homemade mayonnaise
   (page 193) or top quality store-bought
¼ cup sour cream
1 egg
½ cup Pepper Jack cheese, grated
½ cup Monterey Jack cheese, grated
¼ cup Parmesan cheese, grated
¼ cup green onion, minced
½ cup green bell pepper, small dice
2 tsp garlic, minced

2 tsp Old Bay seasoning
2 Tbl Worcestershire sauce
2 Tbl lemon juice, freshly squeezed
1 tsp hot sauce
2 tsp Creole mustard
1 cup corn, freshly cooked or frozen
1 tsp salt
½ tsp black pepper, freshly ground
1 lb crab claw meat, picked clean of all
   shell

1. Preheat oven to 350 degrees.
2. In a large mixing bowl, mix the mayonnaise, sour cream, and egg together. Add the remaining ingredients, except for the crab, and mix until thoroughly blended. Gently fold in the crabmeat.
3. Place in a 1½-quart buttered baking dish and bake 20–25 minutes, until bubbly.
4. Serve with crackers, French-Bread Croutons (page 202), or Herbed-Pita Triangles (page 212).

Spinach-and-Pepper-Jack Dip

Chain restaurants have beaten the spinach-artichoke horse to death. There are no artichokes in this recipe (which is a good thing, since the ingredient listing is rather long), but the chains can't compare with this homemade version.

2 Tbl butter

½ cup onion, minced

¼ cup red bell pepper, medium dice

¼ cup celery, finely chopped

2 tsp garlic, minced

2 tsp salt

1 tsp Creole seasoning (page 205)

1 tsp black pepper, freshly ground

1 tsp dried basil

½ tsp dried oregano

1 lb frozen spinach, thawed, squeezed dry

½ pound cream cheese, softened

¼ cup sour cream

¼ cup homemade mayonnaise
   (page 193) or top quality store-bought

¼ cup milk

2 eggs

1 cup PepperJack cheese, grated

1 Tbl hot sauce

2 tsp Worcestershire sauce

1. Preheat oven to 375 degrees.
2. In a large sauté pan, melt butter over medium heat. Cook the onion, pepper, and celery for 5 minutes. Add the garlic and the seasonings and cook 3–4 minutes more. Stir in the spinach and cook 5 minutes. Remove from the heat and set aside.
3. Place the cream cheese in the bowl of an electric mixer. Using the paddle attachment, beat until smooth. Add the sour cream, mayonnaise, milk, and eggs and blend well. Add the spinach mixture, cheese, hot sauce, and Worcestershire sauce to the bowl, and mix until thoroughly blended.
4. Pour into a 2-quart baking dish and cook 35–40 minutes, until bubbly. Cool slightly before serving.

Four- (or Five-) Cheese Dip

Most hot cheese dips don't use blue cheese . . . not the case here. If you don't like blue cheese, leave it out and step up the amount of one of the other cheeses.

¼ cup unsalted butter
4 Tbl flour
½ cup yellow onion, chopped
¼ cup red bell pepper, small dice
2 tsp garlic
1 tsp Creole seasoning (page 205)
½ tsp salt
½ tsp black pepper, freshly ground
1 cup half-and-half, hot
1 cup chicken broth, hot

½ cup dry sherry
¼ cup cream cheese, softened
¼ cup Parmesan cheese, grated
½ cup sharp Cheddar cheese, grated
¼ cup blue cheese crumbles
¼ cup Pepper Jack cheese, grated
1 Tbl lemon juice, freshly squeezed
1 Tbl parsley, finely chopped
¼ cup green onion, minced

TIP for Entertaining

To keep the phone from ringing off the hook, ask guests for "regrets only."

1. In a medium-sized saucepan, melt the butter over medium heat. Stir in the flour and make a roux. Cook roux five minutes, stirring constantly to prevent burning. Stir in the onion, bell pepper, and garlic, and cook for 2–3 minutes.
2. Using a wire whisk, stir in the seasonings, hot half-and-half, broth, and sherry. Continue to cook over medium heat for 8–9 minutes, stirring often to prevent mixture from sticking.
3. Fold in the cheeses and the lemon juice and stir until cheeses have melted.
4. Garnish with the parsley and the green onion just before serving.
5. Serve warm with tortilla chips or crackers for dipping.

Sin Bread

This is great for a Super Bowl party. Before baking, pop it into the microwave for a few minutes, to take the chill out of the center.

1 loaf round French or sourdough bread
1 Tbsp bacon fat
¼ cup red onion, finely minced
2 tsp garlic, minced
1 Tbl Creole seasoning (page 205)
¼ cup green bell pepper, diced
¼ cup red bell pepper, diced
2 Tbl jalapeños, finely chopped

½ lb cream cheese, softened
¼ lb sharp Cheddar cheese, shredded
¼ lb white Cheddar cheese, shredded
1 cup sour cream
¼ cup green onion, finely chopped
1 tsp Worcestershire sauce
1 tsp hot sauce

1. Preheat oven to 350 degrees.
2. Using a sharp knife, remove a large slice from the top of the bread loaf. Cut out the center of the loaf, leaving a "bowl" with a 2–3-inch thickness of bread around the edges. Dice the bread removed from the center into 1½-inch cubes.
3. Place the bread bowl, the top piece of bread, and the cubed bread on a baking sheet, and toast in the oven.

TIP for Entertaining

Remain calm-stay relaxed while planning and preparing for your party. Your guests will pick up on your outlook and be relaxed too.

4. In a sauté pan, heat the bacon fat over low heat. Cook the onion, garlic, Creole seasoning, and peppers for 3 minutes. Remove from heat.

5. Place the cream cheese in a mixing bowl and beat well until smooth. Stir in all of the remaining ingredients, and the cooked onion mixture.

6. Fill the bread bowl with the cheese mixture. Place the bread "lid" on the loaf and wrap in foil.

7. Bake for 1 hour.

8. Serve with the toasted bread squares.

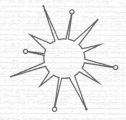

Sauces, Blends, and Extras

Pepper-Jelly Dipping Sauce

Georgia-Peanut Dipping Sauce

Muscadine Dipping Sauce

Raspberry-Mint Dipping Sauce

Creole-Tomato Dipping Sauce

Lemon-Caper Tartar Sauce

Chive-and-Tarragon Sauce

Cucumber-Yogurt Sauce

Plum Dipping Sauce

Seafood Rémoulade Sauce

Roasted Red-Pepper Aioli

Homemade Mayonnaise

Horseradish Mustard

Tabasco-Tartar Sauce

Comeback Sauce

Chantilly Cream

Cocktail Sauce

Blackberry-Tasso Chutney

Fig Butter

French-Bread Croutons

Southwestern Spice

Lamb Rub

Creole Seasoning

Steak Seasoning

Poultry Seasoning

Vegetable Seasoning

Seasoned Flour

Easy Pastry

Pie Dough

Dirty Rice

Lemon-Pepper Dipping Crackers

Herbed-Pita Triangles

Pepper-Jelly Dipping Sauce

Yield: 3 cups

This recipe has multiple uses. It works as a sweet and spicy dipping sauce for the Shrimp Toast (page 8) and Crabmeat Puffs (page 20) in this book, but it also works well as a condiment to be served alongside egg rolls and spring rolls. For a unique and unusual treat, toss a few tablespoons of this sauce with fried popcorn shrimp, fried crawfish tails, or fried calamari.

1 cup water

¼ cup red chili-pepper flakes

1 large red bell pepper, seeds removed

1 Tbl garlic, minced

½ cup rice vinegar

¾ cup corn syrup

1 cup white wine vinegar

1 cup sugar

2 Tbl water

2 Tbl cornstarch

1. Bring the water to a boil in a small saucepan. Stir in the chili flakes and simmer 5 minutes. Strain flakes, set aside, and discard water.

2. Place the bell pepper and the garlic in a small, stainless-steel sauce pan with the vinegars and simmer 5–6 minutes. Allow mixture to cool slightly, then purée in a blender. Return puréed mixture to the saucepan and add the sugar and the corn syrup. Bring the mixture back to a simmer.

3. Dissolve the cornstarch in the water and blend into the bell pepper mixture. Once it returns to a simmer, remove from heat. Stir in the red chili-pepper flakes and chill.

4. May be made a week in advance.

Georgia-Peanut Dipping Sauce

Yield: 3 cups

In addition to accompanying chicken skewers, this can be used in a cold pasta salad with fresh Asian vegetables or a sautéed shrimp pasta with garlic and snow peas.

2 Tbl peanut oil, divided
1 cup unsalted peanuts
1 Tbl shallots, minced
1 Tbl ginger, minced
2 cloves garlic, minced
2 tsp fresh jalapeños, minced
½ cup coconut milk
¼ cup rice vinegar

¼ cup cottonseed oil
¼ cup warm water
2 Tbl soy sauce
1 lime, juiced
½ tsp lime zest
2 Tbl fresh cilantro, chopped
½ tsp salt
¼ tsp cayenne pepper

1. In a skillet, heat 1 Tbl of the peanut oil and sauté the peanuts until golden brown (approximately 4–6 minutes). Drain peanuts on paper towels.
2. Heat the remaining peanut oil and cook the shallots, ginger, garlic, and jalapeños over low heat, 4–5 minutes. Add the coconut milk and vinegar and simmer slowly for 5 more minutes.
3. Place the peanuts into the simmering liquid and continue to cook 5 more minutes. Remove from heat and allow to cool 10 minutes.
4. Transfer mixture to a blender and purée until smooth. Continue to blend, adding in the remaining ingredients. (If the sauce is too thick, add a bit more warm water.)
5. The sauce may be made several days in advance. Store in an airtight container in the refrigerator. Best when served at room temperature.

Muscadine Dipping Sauce

Muscadine jelly is one of the South's greatest treasures.

1 cup muscadine jelly
¼ cup white vinegar
¼ cup Creole mustard
¼ cup horseradish
1 tsp black pepper, freshly ground
1 tsp salt

1. In a medium-sized saucepan over medium heat, melt the jelly with the vinegar and stir until smooth.
2. Remove from heat and stir in the remaining ingredients.

TIP for Entertaining

Never use matching serving pieces. Use pieces found at estate sales to mix it up and add some life-and history-to a table.

Raspberry-Mint Dipping Sauce

In addition to the lamb application, this is a perfect accompaniment to pork and turkey.

1 Tbl olive oil
½ cup shallots, minced
1 Tbl garlic, minced
1 tsp Creole seasoning (page 205)
¼ tsp black pepper, freshly ground
½ cup sherry
2 cups raspberries, fresh or frozen

2 cups chicken broth
1 bay leaf
1 cup mint jelly
½ tsp balsamic vinegar
1 tsp Creole mustard
1 Tbl fresh mint, chopped

1. In a small saucepan, heat olive oil over medium-high heat and cook shallots 3–4 minutes. Stir in garlic and seasonings, and cook 3–4 more minutes, stirring often. Do not let garlic brown. Deglaze with the sherry and reduce by half.
2. Stir in the raspberries, chicken broth, and bay leaf and simmer 15–20 minutes, until reduced by half. Stir in the mint jelly and cook 3 minutes more, stirring constantly.
3. Remove from heat and stir in the vinegar, mustard, and fresh mint.
4. Serve at room temperature.

Substitute chicken base when stock is called for. Canned, non-condensed stock is less salty and has a lighter flavor.

TIP for Entertaining

Creole-Tomato Dipping Sauce

Yield: 1 quart

This sauce is out of this world. It's the perfect sauce to be served with Red-Bean-and-Rice Spring Rolls, but can stand on its own. Multiply the recipe by four and use it as a dip. It's good on burgers and chicken sandwiches, too.

1 Tbl olive oil
2 Tbl green bell pepper, roughly chopped
¼ cup onion, roughly chopped
1 Tbl garlic, minced
¼ cup celery, roughly chopped
2 tsp Creole seasoning (page 205)
1 cup tomatoes, roughly chopped
½ cup white wine
2 cups chicken stock

1 bay leaf
1 tsp dried oregano
1 Tbl fresh thyme, chopped
1 tsp black pepper, freshly ground
½ cup sour cream
¼ cup homemade mayonnaise,
   (page 193) or top quality store-bought
1 tsp lemon juice, freshly squeezed
2 tsp hot sauce

1. In a medium-sized saucepan, heat the olive oil over medium-high heat. Sauté the pepper, onion, garlic, celery, and Creole seasoning for 5 minutes. Add the tomatoes and cook 5 minutes longer. Add the wine and reduce by half. Add the chicken stock, bay leaf, and oregano and simmer 15–20 minutes, or until sauce is thickened.
2. Remove from stove and allow this mixture to cool. Stir in the remaining ingredients.

TIP for Entertaining

Warmth ripens tomatoes, not sunlight. Store tomatoes stem down so they will stay fresher longer.

186

Lemon-Caper Tartar Sauce

Good with fried shrimp, oysters, catfish, or onion rings.

1 cup homemade mayonnaise (page 193)
   or top quality store-bought
1 tsp lemon zest
2 Tbl capers, finely chopped
2 Tbl parsley, freshly chopped
1 Tbl red onion, finely minced
1 Tbl sweet pickle relish
½ tsp Creole seasoning (page 205)
1 Tbl lemon juice, freshly squeezed
½ tsp black pepper, freshly ground

1. Combine all the ingredients and refrigerate for 1–2 hours before using.

Always plan for the unexpected. If your event is outdoors, plan for rain, snow, extreme heat, or cold, and have an alternate location.

TIP for Entertaining

Chive-and-Tarragon Sauce

Yield: 1¼ cups

This is a versatile sauce with an excellent shelf life. It's good with almost any sandwich.

1 cup homemade mayonnaise (page 193)
   or top quality store-bought
1 tsp chives, chopped
1 tsp parsley, chopped
2 tsp tarragon, chopped
¼ tsp garlic, minced

½ tsp black pepper, freshly ground
2 Tbl sour cream
2 Tbl buttermilk
⅛ tsp cayenne pepper
¼ tsp salt

1. Mix together all the ingredients. For the best flavor, prepare and refrigerate a day in advance.

Cucumber-Yogurt Sauce

Good with Smoked-Salmon Spread (page 160), and a great dip on its own. Use it when making gyros.

2 cups plain yogurt (do not use lowfat or
    nonfat)
1 English hothouse cucumber (about 16
    oz), peeled, halved lengthwise,
    and seeded
3 Tbl fresh dill, finely chopped
1 large garlic clove, minced

1. Place strainer over large bowl. Line strainer with 3 layers of cheesecloth. Spoon the yogurt into cheesecloth-lined strainer; let stand at room temperature to drain 3 hours (liquid will drain out and yogurt will thicken). Transfer yogurt to medium bowl; discard liquid. Meanwhile, coarsely grate the cucumber. Place in another strainer; let stand at room temperature until most of liquid drains out, about 3 hours. Discard liquid. Squeeze excess moisture from cucumber. Mix cucumber, dill, and garlic into yogurt. (Can be made 1 day ahead. Cover and refrigerate.) Season to taste with salt and pepper and serve.

Precut veggies and prewashed, precut lettuce are great
time-savers, but to get the freshest flavors, cut your own.

TIP for
Entertaining

Plum Dipping Sauce

This sauce is paired with Shrimp Toast in this book, but can also be used as a glaze for roasting meats, or in a sauté pan with shrimp to be served over rice.

1 cup plum preserves or plum jam	1 tsp fresh ginger, minced
2 Tbl rice wine vinegar	½ tsp garlic, minced
1 Tbl onion, minced	½ tsp jalapeños, minced
1 tsp honey	½ tsp crushed red-pepper flakes

1. In a small saucepan, bring all the ingredients to a boil. Reduce heat and simmer, stirring often, until preserves are melted (approximately 5 minutes). Remove from heat.
2. Let cool to room temperature before serving.
3. Sauce will keep refrigerated in an airtight container for up to 1 week.

TIP for Entertaining

Use an irregularly cut piece of slate as a serving tray.

Seafood Rémoulade Sauce

Yield: 2 cups

This sauce is a hybrid that I developed at the Crescent City Grill years ago. I used to dip fried or boiled shrimp in traditional white rémoulade and then into cocktail sauce. Both flavors are great with seafood, but I could never choose one over the other. Simple solution: Blend the two together.

⅓ cup onion, finely chopped
¼ cup celery, finely chopped
½ cup ketchup
1½ Tbl lemon juice, freshly
   squeezed
1 Tbl prepared horseradish
½ cup homemade mayonnaise
   (page 193) or top quality
   store-bought

1½ Tbl Creole seasoning
   (page 205)
1 tsp Lawry's seasoned salt
½ tsp garlic, minced

1. Place the onion and the celery into a mixing bowl. Add the remaining ingredients and blend well.
2. Rémoulade sauce tastes better if made at least 1 day in advance.

Serve only one type of appetizer per tray.

TIP for
Entertaining

Roasted Red Pepper Aioli

Use a dollop to finish a wide variety of dishes. Some folks like to dip their French fries in it.

2 egg yolks	¾ cup extra-virgin olive oil
1 tsp salt	¼ cup cottonseed oil
1 tsp Dijon mustard	½ cup roasted red bell pepper,
1 tsp garlic, minced	small dice
1 Tbl balsamic vinegar	⅛ tsp black pepper, freshly ground

1. In a medium-sized mixing bowl, vigorously whip together the yolks, salt, mustard, and garlic with a wire whisk. Beat 4–5 minutes, until the yolks become light in color. Add the vinegar, and slowly add the oils, beating constantly until both are incorporated. Fold in the roasted peppers and the black pepper.

2. Best if refrigerated 3 days before using.

Homemade Mayonnaise

Infinitely better than store-bought.

2 egg yolks
1 tsp salt
½ tsp Dijon mustard
1½ tsp lemon juice, freshly squeezed
1 cup cottonseed oil or light vegetable oil
1 tsp white vinegar

1. In a small mixing bowl, whisk together the egg yolks, salt, and mustard. When mixture becomes light in color, add the lemon juice. Slowly drizzle in the oil, whisking constantly. After adding half of the oil, stir in the vinegar. Continue whisking and add the remaining oil.
2. May be held refrigerated for 1 week.

Stir a small amount of rice wine vinegar, lemon juice, or lime juice into commercial mayonnaise to give it a fresh taste. Spices, dill, cilantro, basil, and horseradish are tasty additions, too.

TIP for Entertaining

Horseradish Mustard

This is a versatile sauce with an excellent shelf life. Good with almost any sandwich.

2 Tbl yellow mustard
¼ cup prepared horseradish
¼ cup Dijon mustard
½ cup Creole mustard
2 Tbl honey

2 Tbl bourbon
1 Tbl ketchup
1 Tbl red wine vinegar
1 Tbl parsley, chopped
1 tsp black pepper, freshly ground

1. Mix together all the ingredients. For the best flavor, prepare and refrigerate the mustard 1 day in advance and allow the mustard to get to room temperature before serving.

TIP for Entertaining

Cold canapés are served on buffets, at luncheons, or with cocktails. Hot canapés are served as entreés or used as the foundation for a dish.

Tabasco-Tartar Sauce

The rule on this one is: The hotter, the better. Add more Tabasco if you are brave enough!

1½ cups homemade mayonnaise (page 193) or top quality store-bought

¼ cup sweet pickle relish, drained

1 Tbl yellow mustard

2 Tbl capers, rinsed well and chopped

2 Tbl green olives, chopped

1½ tsp black pepper, freshly ground

1½ tsp garlic, minced

½ tsp garlic salt

1½ tsp parsley, chopped

1 Tbl lemon juice, freshly squeezed

2 Tbl Tabasco sauce

1. Combine all the ingredients, mix well, and refrigerate 4–6 hours before serving.

For easy olive-pitting, gently whack the olive with the wide side of a chef's knife and remove the pit.

TIP for Entertaining

Comeback Sauce

The ultimate Mississippi condiment, invented in the Greek restaurants of Jackson, Mississippi. At our restaurant, we receive more comments on Comeback Sauce than on any other item. People love it. It is versatile and it is good. Use it as a salad dressing or as a fried-seafood condiment. I enjoy dipping crackers into it; it's good on burgers, and it is absolutely the best condiment to serve with onion rings.

1 cup homemade mayonnaise (page 193)
   or top quality store-bought
½ cup ketchup
½ cup chili sauce
½ cup cottonseed oil
½ cup yellow onion, grated
3 Tbl lemon juice, freshly squeezed

2 Tbl garlic, minced
1 Tbl paprika
1 Tbl water
1 Tbl Worcestershire sauce
1 tsp black pepper
½ tsp dry mustard
1 tsp salt

1. Combine all the ingredients in a food processor and mix well.

Chantilly Cream

With a tip of the toque to the master—Chef Paul Prudhomme.

½ cup heavy cream
1 tsp vanilla
1 tsp Grand Marnier
1 tsp brandy
3 Tbl sugar
2 Tbl sour cream

1. Combine the cream, vanilla, Grand Marnier, and brandy in a mixing bowl and using an electric mixer, whip for three minutes. Add in the sugar and sour cream and continue beating on medium until it looks like whipped cream. Do not overwhip.

Cocktail Sauce

1½ cups ketchup
3 Tbl fresh lemon juice
2 tsp Worcestershire sauce
¼ cup horseradish, prepared
½ tsp black pepper, freshly ground
1½ tsp salt

1. Combine all ingredients and mix well. Refrigerate 2 hours before serving.

TIP for Entertaining

Use small picture frames for name cards. You can also take a Polaroid picture of the guest as he or she arrives and place it in a typical name-card holder at the guest's seat. Have the guest make a funny face to add a little life to the sit-down portion of dinner.

Blackberry-Tasso Chutney

This chutney offers big, bold flavors with multiple uses. Serve it with duck, venison, pork, or savory bread pudding. Leave out the tasso and serve it over ice cream.

1 cup shallots, finely chopped
1 cup onion, medium dice
½ cup tasso, minced
1 Tbl unsalted butter
6 oz fresh blackberries (or frozen, 2 cups, unthawed)
¼ cup sugar

½ cup blackberry preserves
2 Tbl cider vinegar
1 Tbl cracked black pepper
1 Tbl ginger, minced
1 cinnamon stick
½ tsp Creole seasoning (page 205)

1. In a 1½-quart heavy saucepan, cook the shallots, onion, and tasso in the butter over moderate heat, stirring occasionally, until golden, 3–5 minutes. Stir in the remaining ingredients and simmer, uncovered, stirring occasionally, until berries burst and chutney is thickened, approximately 20 minutes.
2. Cool to room temperature.
3. Note: Chutney can be made 1 week ahead and chilled, covered.

Homemade pickles and relishes add a nice touch to meat dishes.

TIP for Entertaining

Fig Butter

This recipe should be made and stored in your refrigerator. Never, ever be without it. If there's a fire at my house—I'm grabbing the wife, the kids, a few family photos, the dog, and the container of fig butter in the fridge. To me, nothing tastes better when spread on homemade biscuits, toast, or croissants. It goes fast!

1½ cups fig preserves
⅛ tsp cinnamon
Pinch of nutmeg
1 tsp vanilla extract
¼ cup unsalted butter, softened

1. Place half of the fig preserves, the spices, the vanilla, and the butter in a food processor. Purée until smooth. Add the remaining fig preserves, and pulse 6–7 times, just enough to slightly break up any large pieces of fig.
2. Store in an airtight container in the refrigerator.

Never overmix biscuit or cookie dough.
Be gentle. Less is more.

TIP for Entertaining

French-Bread Croutons

These are better than crackers when serving dips and spreads. They're great with cheeses, too.

¼ cup salted butter
⅓ cup extra-virgin olive oil
1 loaf French bread, cut crosswise
   into ½-inch-thick circles

1. Preheat oven to 325 degrees.
2. Melt the butter and the olive oil together. Arrange slices of French-bread circles onto a wax-lined baking sheet and brush tops evenly with the butter mixture. Toast until golden brown. Cool and store in an airtight container until needed.

TIP for Entertaining

When serving finger foods, cocktail napkins are a must. Place the side of a cocktail glass on top of a small pile of napkins, bear down, and turn the glass in a twisting motion to create a nice presentation.

Southwestern Spice

This one is great on skirt steak or chicken.

2 Tbl chili powder
1 Tbl ground cumin
2 tsp ground coriander
1½ tsp dried oregano
1 tsp paprika
1 tsp black pepper, freshly ground
2 Tbl garlic salt
1 Tbl onion powder

1. Combine all ingredients.

Overmixing ground beef when making patties will result in dry burgers with sub-par texture. Be gentle. Never flatten them with a spatula during cooking.

TIP for
Entertaining

Lamb Rub

This rub works great on venison, too.

2 Tbl lemon pepper

1 Tbl dried oregano

1 Tbl dried basil

1 Tbl black pepper, freshly ground

1 Tbl brown sugar

1 Tbl garlic salt

½ tsp cinnamon

1 tsp dried, ground rosemary

1 Tbl paprika

1 Tbl onion powder

1. Combine all the ingredients and store in an airtight container.

TIP for Entertaining

Use cloves to counteract the odors of other dishes being cooked. Place a dozen cloves in a small pan of boiling water and let it simmer. The pleasant aroma will offset most strong odors.

Creole Seasoning

Yield: 1 cup

Over the course of my twenty-five-year restaurant career, I have used this seasoning more than any other ingredient. It is one of the earliest recipes I developed. I use it on all types of seafood, and as I would use salt on many others.

½ cup Lawry's seasoned salt
2 Tbl onion powder
2 Tbl paprika
1 Tbl cayenne pepper
1 Tbl white pepper

1 Tbl plus 1 tsp garlic powder
1 Tbl black pepper
1 tsp dry mustard
1 tsp dried oregano
1 tsp dried thyme

1. Combine all the ingredients.

Fresh fish should be cooked immediately.

TIP for Entertaining

Steak Seasoning

This seasoning works well with steak, hamburger, lamb, and meatloaf. Always have it handy.

½ cup Lawry's seasoned salt
⅓ cup black pepper
¼ cup lemon pepper
2 Tbl garlic salt
2 Tbl granulated garlic
1 Tbl onion powder

1. Combine all and mix well. Store in an airtight container.

TIP for Entertaining

It is important to let a roast rest before carving. The juices that have moved to the outer edges during cooking will retreat back into the meat. If a roast is carved too soon, most of the flavor will spill out onto the carving board.

Poultry Seasoning

Yield: Approximately 1¼ cup

Use this to season chicken before grilling, baking, frying, or roasting. It can also be used to season flour for fried chicken. It's good for turkey, too.

¼ cup Lawry's seasoned salt
¼ cup garlic powder
¼ cup white pepper
¼ cup lemon pepper
¼ cup celery salt

1. Combine all the ingredients and mix well. Store in an airtight container.

Vegetable Seasoning

Yield: Approximately ¼ cup

2 Tbl dry ranch dressing mix
1 Tbl Lawry's seasoned salt
1 Tbl onion powder
2 tsp paprika
2 tsp celery salt
1 tsp black pepper, freshly ground
1 tsp salt
1 tsp garlic powder

1. Combine all the ingredients and mix thoroughly.

Seasoned Flour

Yield: 2 cups

Keep this one in your cupboard at all times.

3 cups all-purpose flour
4 Tbl Creole seasoning (page 205)

1. Mix flour and seasoning thoroughly.

Easy Pastry

**Yield: 35-40 small pastries or
2 pie crusts (top and bottom)**

This pastry is easy to work with, yet delicate. It's possibly the most versatile pastry going. It holds for four or five days in the refrigerator, freezes well and fries well, and works great in both sweet and savory applications.

1 cup butter, softened
1 eight-oz package cream cheese,
   softened

½ tsp salt
2 cups flour

1. By hand, or using a paddle attachment on an electric mixer, combine all the ingredients to form a soft dough. Do not overmix.
2. Wrap the dough well and refrigerate 10–12 hours before using.
3. When ready to use, remove dough from refrigerator and allow it to sit at room temperature 10–15 minutes before using.

Pie Dough

Yield: 2 crusts

Make sure that the shortening is cold. Don't overwork it. Dryer climates might require a little more liquid.

2 cups flour
1 cup shortening
¼ tsp salt
1 egg
⅓ cup milk

1. Blend the first 3 ingredients together with a pastry-cutter or a fork. Separately, beat the egg and the milk together. Slowly add egg/milk mixture to flour mixture, one tablespoon at a time, until pie dough becomes moist. Divide in half and shape into a ball. Wrap and refrigerate 1 hour before rolling.

2. To roll out dough: Remove dough disk from refrigerator. If stiff and cold, let stand until dough is cool but malleable.

3. Using a floured rolling pin, roll dough disk on a lightly floured surface from the center out in each direction, forming a 12-inch circle. To transfer dough, carefully roll it around the rolling pin, then lift and unroll dough, centering it in an ungreased nine-inch pie plate.

To keep hot foods hot, warm the plates. When serving gravy in a gravy boat, pour hot water into it, to warm the boat, first. When serving ice cream or sorbet, chill the bowls.

TIP for Entertaining

Dirty Rice

This is a great side dish, as well as a major component in other recipes in this book.

2 oz ground pork

2 oz ground beef

1 Tbl bacon fat

1 bay leaf

1 Tbl poultry seasoning
   (page 207)

1 tsp dry mustard

½ cup onion, medium dice

¼ cup celery, medium dice

¼ cup bell pepper, medium dice

2 tsp garlic, minced

1 cup rice

2 Tbl butter

2 cups pork stock, hot (use 2 cups
   water and 1 Tbl ham base)

1. Brown the ground pork and beef in the bacon fat.
2. Add the seasonings and veggies and cook 10 minutes.
3. Stir in the rice, butter, and hot stock, lower heat, cover, and simmer 18 minutes.

Lemon-Pepper Dipping Crackers

Good with cold dips.

1 box Triscuit crackers
½ cup salted butter, melted
2 tsp lemon pepper
1 tsp garlic, minced

1. Preheat oven to 350 degrees.
2. Place the crackers in a large mixing bowl. Drizzle with melted butter and toss with lemon pepper and garlic. Spread crackers on a baking sheet and toast 5 minutes.

When using different types of meat for meatloaf, have your butcher grind it twice for ideal texture and mixing. Always use your hands to mix.

TIP for Entertaining

Herbed Pita Triangles

Yield: 40 triangles

These triangles are great served with hot dips.

½ cup olive oil
1½ tsp dried basil
½ tsp dried oregano
⅛ tsp dried rosemary

¼ tsp black pepper, freshly ground
5 fresh pita breads
½–¾ tsp garlic salt

1. Preheat oven to 350 degrees.
2. Combine the oil with the dried herbs and pepper.
3. Arrange the pita bread on a baking sheet pan. Brush the tops of the pita with the herbed oil mixture and then sprinkle with the garlic salt. Bake 8–12 minutes. Remove from oven and cut each pita into 8 triangles.
4. Serve warm. If preparing in advance, wrap the triangles in foil and hold in a warming oven at 170 degrees.

TIP for Entertaining

Hors d'oeuvres are finger foods or small portions served with cocktails before a meal. An "appetizer" is a small course served before a meal or as a first course.

Had I Known You Were Coming (In So Late) I Would Have Baked You a Cake

Cooking for company can be a nerve-wracking experience. It takes a few parties for one to gain his or her shindig sea legs. Nerves are the main culprit, with inexperience coming in a close second. A first-time host might try to experiment on his guests; the experienced party-giver will never serve a new dish to company.

My newlywed wife had never cooked for company and had never baked a cake. Knowing that we had a guest sleeping over and that yellow cake with chocolate icing was my favorite, she went to work. Her initial attempt at baking is legendary.

First, I must explain that even though I am a highly trained food-service professional, she doesn't want me in the kitchen while she is cooking. I try to offer helpful hints. She shuns them. Her inaugural cake project was doomed from the start.

Mistake No. 1: She used cake pans that were too small. The cake rose unevenly, forming a rounded top. Both layers looked like miniature versions of the Superdome. If I were in the kitchen, I would have told her to cut the cake horizontally to flatten the top out so it could be stacked and iced. But I was hiding in the den.

Mistake No. 2: She didn't let the cake cool. Once again, had I been in the kitchen, I would have explained the theory of cooling a cake on a rack. She placed the least-rounded cake on the bottom, and the most severely domed cake on top.

Mistake No. 3: She iced the cake immediately, saving most of the icing for the top of the cake. She then placed the hot, iced cake under the glass cake display.

She called me into the kitchen to see her creation. Of course, it was hard to see through all of the steam inside of the glass, but as I drew closer, things got weird. As we stood there looking at my wife's first baking project, it began to move. I kid you not.

"It's alive!" I yelled.

We watched, puzzled, as a crack began forming down the center of the cake, running from one side to the other. The weight of the icing pulled the hot cake from its center and split it down the middle. The hot icing oozed into the crack and re-iced the cake instantly. We stood in awe, looking at her cake, which had instantly transformed into two rounded chocolate humps with a crack in the center. It looked like a big, brown butt. I dubbed it the butt cake. We both laughed (the key word in that sentence is "both").

I left the butt cake under the glass dome for viewing by visiting friends. When anyone came to our house, I would say, "Come see the butt cake." I considered it a museum piece, and never let anyone cut into it.

It stayed under the glass dome for so long that it began to grow a freaky green fuzz. Eventually it turned into a science project and became completely covered with green mold. The icing hardened and the cake fossilized. Some homemakers develop a green thumb; my wife created a green butt.

Enter the dinner guest. Our friend Glen was in town for a business meeting and bunking in the guest room. He was single, and decided to visit old friends at a local neighborhood bar. We were newlyweds, so we stayed home and . . . didn't eat cake.

Sometime after 2:00 A.M. we heard the door alarm signaling Glen's entrance. When we awoke later that morning, Glen was gone.

When we walked into the kitchen, it was obvious what had occurred just hours before. Glen had entered the house after a very socially active night—skipping dinner, opting for a liquid diet—with a strong craving.

Unfortunately, it was a craving for cake.

Not wanting to turn the lights on and disturb the owners of the house, he decided to pour a glass of milk and eat a piece of cake in the dark. Because it was dark, Glen didn't know that the cake on the glass pedestal was the aforementioned three-month-old, green, fuzzy butt cake.

A plate with a large slice of butt cake sat on the counter next to the sink. A fork was on the floor, the glass of milk was half empty. The bite of butt cake had been spit out into the sink along with the milk, the liquid diet, and various and sundry other items that can't be described in a family cookbook.

My wife has baked many cakes over the last thirteen years, all of which have been eaten in a matter of days, and none of which have grown hair or moved.

Glen married, settled down, and became a father. He has been able to keep off the pounds that most married men add on. He has my wife to thank for that. In one dark, fateful night, she cured his midnight-snack cravings forever.

Sweets

Miniature Strawberry Shortcakes

S'more Squares

Miniature Fried Peach Pies

Sweet-Potato Brownies

Strawberry-Filled Strawberry Tarts with Chantilly Cream

Peach-Pecan Ice-Cream Sandwiches

Linda's Never-Fail Cheesecakes

Mini Pecan Tartlets

Bourbon-Pecan Truffles

Miniature Banana-Nut Muffins

White-Trash Apricot Tarts

Gingerbread

Miniature Strawberry Shortcakes

I love strawberry shortcake, but never see it at a party. Some might think it's too simple, others might think it's too casual. Still others might not serve it because it is hard to eat in a cocktail setting. It's true, strawberry shortcake is simple and casual, but most of all, it's good. This recipe takes care of the hard-to-eat-at-a-cocktail-party problem by making it a hand-held treat.

SHORTCAKE DOUGH
2 cups self-rising flour
2 Tbl sugar
¼ cup unsalted butter, cut into small
   pieces and chilled
¾ cup buttermilk
2 Tbl butter, melted
2 Tbl sugar

FOR THE BERRIES
½ cup sugar

2 Tbl lemon juice
1 tsp vanilla
1 cup strawberries, small dice
3 Tbl cold water
2 Tbl cornstarch

WHIPPED CREAM TOPPING
¼ cup cream cheese, softened
2 Tbl sour cream
2 Tbl powdered sugar
2 Tbl heavy whipping cream

TIP for Entertaining

For perfect whipped cream, make sure the beaters, mixing bowl, and cream are kept cold until just before mixing.

1. Preheat oven to 375 degrees.
2. In a food processor, combine the flour and sugar and pulse to mix. Add the butter pieces and pulse until the mixture resembles bread crumbs. Transfer mixture to large mixing bowl and make a well in the center. Pour buttermilk into the well and gently blend together the dough, being careful not to overmix.
3. Allow dough to set for 10 minutes and then turn it out onto floured surface. Gently knead the dough for 1–2 minutes, then roll out to a ¾-inch thickness. Cut 1½-inch circles from the dough and place on an ungreased baking sheet. Brush tops with the melted butter and sprinkle with the sugar.
4. Bake for 12–15 minutes.
5. In a small sauté pan, heat the sugar, vanilla, and lemon juice and allow to melt. Add the strawberries and cook 5 minutes.
6. Mix together the cold water and cornstarch and stir it into the strawberries. Allow berries to thicken. Remove from heat and chill mixture completely.
7. Whip the cream cheese, sour cream, and powdered sugar until smooth and light. Add the heavy cream and whip for 1 more minute.
8. To build shortcakes, split the cooled shortcakes with a knife. Fill with 1–2 tsp of the strawberry filling. Top with a dollop of whipped cream.

S'more Squares

I don't like s'mores. When I went to Chef Linda Nance, recipe tester, with the idea for this recipe, I told her why I didn't like s'mores (the marshmallows burn, the chocolate never melts, the graham cracker crumbles), she went to work. Her efforts produced one of best and most inventive desserts I've seen in a long time. It is her favorite recipe in the book.

2 cups graham cracker crumbs
1 cup sugar
¾ cup melted butter
1 lb semisweet chocolate
½ cup sugar

1½ cups heavy whipping cream
1½ tsp vanilla extract
1 seven-oz jar Marshmallow Fluff
3 cups marshmallows

CRUST
1. Preheat oven to 375 degrees.
2. Spray the inside of a 9 x 13-inch baking sheet with nonstick cooking spray. In a bowl, combine the graham cracker crumbs, sugar, and melted butter. Press mixture firmly into the sprayed pie tin, covering bottom and sides.
3. Bake for 6–8 minutes. Set aside to cool.

TIP for Entertaining

Run a knife in a zigzag pattern through the batter in a cake pan to remove the air bubbles.

FILLING

1. Combine the chocolate, sugar, heavy whipping cream, and vanilla, and melt in a double-boiler. Stir until melted. Pour two thirds of the chocolate mixture onto the crust, distributing it evenly. Set in refrigerator and allow this layer to harden while preparing the second layer.

2. For the second layer, add the Marshmallow Fluff to the remaining chocolate mixture and mix with an electric mixer until smooth. Pour this mixture on top of the firm chocolate layer and spread it out evenly.

3. Using a wet, sharp knife, cut the marshmallows into thin disks (three disks per marshmallow). Arrange the disks on top of the chocolate marshmallow layer. Refrigerate for 1 hour.

4. After the squares have been refrigerated, brown the marshmallows underneath a hot broiler. Allow to cool once more.

5. Dip a sharp knife into hot water and carefully cut into squares.

6. Refrigerate at least 1 hour.

Miniature Fried Peach Pies

Yield: 24-26 mini pies

Here is a true Southern dessert staple. These pies work well with apples, too.*

SWEET PIE DOUGH
8 Tbl unsalted butter, room temperature
1½ Tbl granulated sugar
⅛ tsp salt
1 large egg
1½ cups all-purpose flour
2 Tbl ice water

FILLING
1 Tbl unsalted butter
½ lb frozen peaches, thawed, or 1 cup
  fresh peaches, small dice

3 Tbl granulated sugar
¼ cup peach jam or preserves
Pinch of cayenne pepper
1 tsp cinnamon
2 tsp cornstarch
1 Tbl peach schnapps
1 Tbl sugar
½ tsp cinnamon

Vegetable oil for deep frying

1. To prepare the pie dough, beat together the butter, sugar, and salt for 3 minutes on medium speed in the bowl of an electric mixer. Add the egg and beat for 30 more seconds. Add the flour and water and beat for 15 more seconds. Turn off the machine, scrape down the sides of the bowl, and beat again for 10 seconds.

TIP for Entertaining

Use icing as soon as it is made; it becomes stiff quickly.
Use an icing spatula and work fast.

2. Scoop up the dough with your hands and form into a 1-inch-thick disk. Wrap in plastic and refrigerate for at least 1 hour.

3. To prepare the filling, melt the butter over medium-high heat in a sauté pan. Sauté the peaches and sugar until sugar is dissolved, approximately 2 minutes. Add the preserves, cayenne, and cinnamon; cook, stirring frequently, for 3 minutes.

4. Dissolve the cornstarch in the schnapps and stir into hot peach mixture. Remove from heat and cool.

5. On a lightly floured surface, roll out the dough into a 16 x 11-inch rectangle about ⅛-inch thick. Cut out 3½-inch circles and place 2 tsps of filling in the center of each dough circle. Fold the circles in half and pinch the edges together. Refrigerate pies for 30 minutes before frying.

6. Heat 2½ inches of vegetable oil to 350 degrees in a heavy 4-quart saucepan. Fry pies 4 or 6 at a time until golden brown, 1½–2 minutes per batch. Drain on paper towels.

7. Keep warm in a 200-degree oven until all pies are fried. Serve immediately.

* If substituting apples for peaches, use apple jelly instead of peach preserves and apple brandy in place of peach schnapps.

Sweet Potato Brownies

If you don't like sweet potatoes, don't worry, you'll love these. If you don't like brownies, have no fear, you'll love these. If you like sweet potatoes and brownies—get ready for an amazing treat!

½ lb butter
2 cups sugar
1½ cups flour
1 tsp salt
4 eggs
2 tsp vanilla
2 cups sweet potatoes, grated

1 cups pecans, toasted

GLAZE
2 Tbl butter
¼ cup orange juice
1 tsp cinnamon
1 cup confectioners' sugar

1. Preheat oven to 350 degrees.
2. In the bowl of an electric mixer, cream together the butter and the sugar until light and fluffy. Add the remaining ingredients in order, stirring after each is added.
3. Pour into a buttered and floured 9 x 12-inch baking sheet.
4. Bake for 30–40 minutes.
5. Allow brownies to cool completely before cutting.
6. Melt the butter and add the remaining ingredients. Let cool. Glaze brownies after they have been cut.

TIP for Entertaining

Sifting dry ingredients onto wax paper makes it easier to pour the ingredients into a mixing bowl.

Strawberry-Filled Strawberry Tarts with Chantilly Cream

Yield: 16 pies

This recipe has its roots in my hero Paul Prudhomme's strawberry pie.

16 premade frozen mini tart shells
3 cups strawberries, sliced
½ cup sugar
¼ cup water

1 package gelatin
8 whole strawberries, hulls
  removed, cut in half

1. Preheat oven to 350 degrees.
2. Bake tart shells for 12–15 minutes, until completely done. Cool before filling with strawberry mixture.
3. Purée the 3 cups sliced strawberries and the sugar.
4. Place strawberry mixture in a saucepan, add the water, and boil for 3 minutes, stirring frequently. Transfer mixture to mixing bowl and add the gelatin, mixing thoroughly.
5. Cool to room temperature.
6. Place half a strawberry in each cooked tart shell and fill shells with the strawberry mixture. Refrigerate 3–4 hours before serving.
7. Top with Chantilly Cream (page 197) just before serving.

If the fruit for cobblers appears too juicy, add an extra tablespoon of flour or cornstarch to the fruit before cooking.

TIP for Entertaining

Peach-Pecan Ice-Cream Sandwiches

This recipe is 100 percent Chef Linda Nance. Although a native of California, she has adopted the South as her home, and can now pronounce "pecan" with a Southern drawl that would make Scarlett O'Hara proud. (It's *puh-kahn*, not *pee-can*!)

PECAN SANDIES FOR ICE-CREAM SANDWICHES

1 cup pecans, toasted

2 cups all-purpose flour

1 cup (2 sticks) unsalted butter, softened

⅔ cup confectioners' sugar

2 tsp vanilla extract

1 tsp salt

½ tsp baking powder

PEACH ICE CREAM *(Yield: 1 quart)*

2 cups peaches, fresh, peeled (or 2 cups frozen)

¾ cup sugar

1 Tbl lemon juice

2 Tbl peach schnapps

½ vanilla bean

1 cup heavy cream

½ cup milk

2 egg yolks

TIP for Entertaining

Never substitute milk for cream when making ice cream.

228

1. In a food processor, pulse the nuts with ¼ cup of the flour. Set aside.
2. Using an electric mixer, beat the butter and sugar until creamy and smooth, approximately 2 minutes. Add the vanilla and beat well. Sift together the remaining 1¾ cups flour, the salt, and the baking powder, and add it to the dough, mixing until just combined. Stir in the nut mixture. Form the dough into a disk, wrap in plastic, and chill for at least 3 hours.
3. Preheat oven to 325 degrees.
4. Roll out the dough to a ⅛-inch thickness and, using a round, 2-inch cookie cutter, cut out cookies. Place on an ungreased baking sheet and bake for 14–16 minutes.
5. Remove and cool completely.
6. To assemble ice cream sandwiches, place a 1-oz scoop of ice cream between 2 pecan sandies. Keep frozen until ready to serve.
7. In a bowl, combine the peaches, ¼ cup sugar, the lemon juice, and the peach schnapps. Cover and refrigerate 2–3 hours or overnight, stirring occasionally.
8. Remove the peach mixture from refrigerator and drain the juice, reserving in a cup. Return peaches to refrigerator.
9. Split the vanilla bean lengthwise, and combine it with remaining sugar, heavy cream, and milk in a small saucepan. Heat just until it just begins to boil.
10. In a bowl, whisk egg yolks. While whisking, stream in about ⅓ of the boiled cream mixture. Stir well. Add egg mixture to cream mixture. Return to heat and continue stirring. Mixture will thicken as it returns to a boil. Remove from heat and strain into a bowl set over ice. Add the reserved peach juice.
11. Transfer the mixture to an ice-cream maker and freeze according to manufacturer's instructions. After the ice cream begins to stiffen, add the peaches and continue to freeze until done.

Linda's Never-Fail Cheesecakes

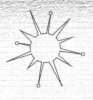

Linda Nance is the master of cheesecake. A springform pan is a must. You can use one of these fillings or let your imagination do the work and develop your own version.

BASIC CHEESECAKE
2 lb cream cheese, room
    temperature
1 cup sugar
Pinch salt
5 eggs plus 4 egg yolks
2 tsp vanilla extract

¾ cup heavy cream

CRUST
1½ cups graham cracker crumbs
½ cup sugar
¾ cup butter, melted

1. Preheat oven to 275 degrees.
2. Place softened cream cheese in large mixing bowl and beat, using paddle attachment on medium speed, until VERY smooth. Scrape sides and beat again to ensure there are no lumps.
3. Add the sugar and salt and mix well. Add in the eggs and the yolks a few at a time, allowing them to incorporate well before adding more.
4. Place the mixer on slow speed and add the vanilla and the cream. As soon as the cream is incorporated, stop mixing.
5. Combine the crumbs and the sugar and mix by hand Add the butter in stages, mixing well before each addition.
6. Evenly distribute the crust in a 9-inch springform pan, pressing it firmly on the bottom of the pan and building crust up 2 inches on the sides of the pan.
7. Pour in the cheesecake batter and bake for 1–1½ hours. The cheesecake should jiggle slightly when tapped.

8. Remove and cool, then refrigerate overnight before serving.
9. To cut, run a thin knife under hot water before cutting each slice.

PUMPKIN CHEESECAKE:

1. Substitute brown sugar for white sugar.
2. Substitute pumpkin purée for heavy cream.
3. Add 2 tsp pumpkin spice.

LEMON-BLUEBERRY CHEESECAKE:

1. After filling is prepared, gently fold in 2 tsp lemon zest and 1½ cups fresh or frozen blueberries.

PEANUT BUTTER AND CHOCOLATE CHEESECAKE:

1. In the crust, replace ½ cup of the graham cracker crumbs with ½ cup finely ground peanuts.
2. When making the filling, use 1½ pounds cream cheese. When the filling is prepared, divide it in half. Beat ½ cup peanut butter into one-half of the filling. Fold 4 oz melted semisweet chocolate into the other half. Alternate filling the crust with the 2 different fillings.

SUMMER PEACHES-AND-CREAM CHEESECAKE:

1. Replace ½ lb of the cream cheese with 8 oz of sour cream.
Add in 1½ cups fresh peaches, peeled and diced, and ¼ cup peach schnapps.

For a fresh dessert presentation, serve fruit sorbet
in an orange or lemon shell.

TIP for
Entertaining

Mini Pecan Tartlets

These are rich and nutty, like your eccentric uncle. They must be held and served at room temperature.

SWEET TART DOUGH
2 cups confectioners' sugar
1 cup unsalted butter
1 tsp vanilla extract
3 cups all-purpose flour
½ tsp salt
1 egg

FILLING
1 cup unsalted butter
1½ cups brown sugar
¼ cup white sugar
½ cup honey
¼ tsp fine salt
⅓ cup heavy cream
4½ cups pecan pieces

1. Preheat oven to 325 degrees.
2. To make the sweet dough: Place the sugar, butter, and vanilla extract in the bowl of an electric mixer. With the paddle attachment, beat the ingredients until creamy. Add the flour and the salt and mix until just combined. Add the egg and mix until just combined (this can also be done in a food processor). Form a disk out of the dough, wrap in plastic wrap, and refrigerate for about half an hour.

TIP for Entertaining

Warm cookies taste better than cold. Heat releases the flavor of chocolate and nuts. Warm room-temperature cookies in the microwave for a few seconds or in a 300-degree oven for approximately five minutes.

3. When dough is slightly chilled, place on a lightly floured surface. Roll dough out in a rectangular shape, approximately 11 x 15 inches in size. Transfer dough to a 9 x 13 baking sheet and gently press dough into bottom and sides of the pan (dough should come up the sides of the pan about 1 inch).

4. Refrigerate dough 30 minutes and bake for 10 minutes. While crust is cooling, prepare the filling.

5. While the pastry is cooling, combine the butter, brown sugar, white sugar, honey, and salt in a large pot over high heat. Boil 6 minutes. Remove from the heat and carefully stir in the cream. (The mixture will boil up while you're adding the cream, so be very careful during this step not to burn yourself.)

6. Add the pecans and mix thoroughly. Pour the filling evenly over the baked pastry. Bake for 20 minutes until golden brown. Cool completely before cutting into squares.

Bourbon-Pecan Truffles

Yield: 20-25 truffles

You can leave the alcohol out, but the chocolate should stay.

8 oz bittersweet or semisweet chocolate, chopped

½ cup heavy cream

2 Tbl butter

¼ cup corn syrup

2 Tbl bourbon

¾ cup toasted, chopped pecans, divided

1. Using a stainless-steel bowl as a double-boiler, place the chopped chocolate in the bowl over a pot of boiling water, melting the chocolate. Do not stir the chocolate while it is melting. In a separate saucepan, bring the cream to a boil. Pour boiling cream over the chocolate. Whip until smooth.
2. Stir in the butter, bourbon, and corn syrup and cool to 80 degrees, using a candy thermometer to check the temperature.
3. In the bowl of an electric mixer, beat with the whip attachment on high until the mixture lightens in color and becomes fluffy. Remove bowl from mixer.
4. Using a spatula, fold in half of the nuts.
5. Using your hands, form the chocolate mixture into even-sized truffles, 1 inch in diameter.
6. When completely cool, roll the truffles in the remaining chopped nuts, coating thoroughly. Refrigerate in a tightly sealed container to store, but the truffles are best when they sit at room temperature 20–30 minutes before serving.

TIP for Entertaining

To make chocolate curls, use a vegetable peeler and a block of chocolate. Serve them alongside the Bourbon-Pecan Truffles.

Miniature Banana-Nut Muffins

Yield: 24 miniature muffins

These are perfect for breakfast, brunch, or a snack.

2 cups flour
¾ cups sugar
1 Tbl baking powder
½ tsp nutmeg
½ cup toasted walnuts, finely chopped
¼ tsp salt

1 egg
½ cup whipping cream
1 medium-sized mashed banana (about 1 cup)
⅓ cup butter, melted

1. Preheat oven to 350 degrees.
2. In one mixing bowl, combine the flour, sugar, baking powder, nutmeg, walnuts, and salt.
3. In another bowl, blend the remaining ingredients together well. Fold the wet ingredients into the dry. Do not overmix.
4. Use the mix to fill nonstick miniature muffin tins ¾ full.
5. Bake for 14–16 minutes.

Black bananas make the best banana bread. Freeze and save for baking later.

TIP for Entertaining

White-Trash Apricot Tarts

The brown butter in the recipe gives these tarts a unique and appealing flavor.

16 premade mini frozen tart shells

FILLING
¾ cup butter
1½ cups apricot preserves

¼ cup honey
1 tsp vanilla
1 cup dried apricots, chopped small
2 eggs
3 Tbl flour

1. Preheat oven to 350 degrees.
2. Par-bake the mini tart shells for 7 minutes.
3. For the filling, melt the butter in a small aluminum saucepan and cook until the butter begins to brown. Stir in the preserves, honey, vanilla, and dried apricots. Remove mixture from heat.
4. In a separate bowl, combine the eggs and the flour and beat until smooth. Slowly add the hot butter mixture, stirring constantly. Fill the tart shell and bake 12 minutes.
5. Cool and serve topped with Chantilly Cream (page 197).

TIP for Entertaining

Covering freshly sliced apples or pears with fresh grapefruit juice or diluted lemon juice will prevent browning.

Gingerbread

I have loved gingerbread since I was a child. For some reason, it's not offered as much as it used to be. I am on a mission to change that trend.

1 stick unsalted butter
1 cup brown sugar
3 large eggs
2 cups all-purpose flour
2 tsp ground ginger
1½ tsp baking soda
1 tsp cinnamon
½ tsp salt
½ tsp ground cloves
¼ tsp nutmeg, freshly grated

1 cup molasses
1 cup hard cider
Apple Icing for topping

APPLE ICING
2 Tbl butter
1 cup apple, peeled, small dice
¼ tsp cinnamon
½ cup hard cider
1½ cups confectioners' sugar

1. Grease a 13 x 9-inch cake pan and line with parchment paper that has also been greased.
2. In a large bowl, cream together the butter and sugar. Beat in the eggs one at a time. In a second bowl, sift together the next 7 dry ingredients. In a third bowl, combine the molasses and hard cider and stir to dissolve. Add the dry ingredients and cider mixture alternately to the egg mixture, beating after the addition of each.
3. Pour into the prepared pan and bake in a 350-degree oven until puffed and set, approximately 35 minutes.
4. Remove from the oven and let cool in the pan on a wire rack.
5. Cut into squares and top with Apple Icing.
6. Melt the butter over medium heat and cook the apples for 5 minutes. Stir in the cinnamon and cider and cook 5 more minutes, until most of the liquid is cooked out. Remove from heat and stir in the sugar. Cool completely before topping gingerbread.

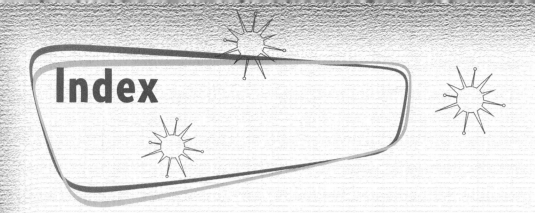

Index

Walnuts
  Cajun-Spiced Nuts, 105
  Miniature Banana-Nut Muffins, 235
Whipped Cream, 220

Yogurt-Cucumber Sauce, 189

Zucchini
  Curried-Crab Dip with Vegetable Fritters,
    150–51
  Marinated and Roasted Vegetables, 50
  Summer Garden Dip, 162